101 Ways to Learn Vocabulary

101 Ways to Learn Vocabulary

Joan D. Berbrich, Ph.D.

Author of other books published by Amsco
WIDE WORLD OF WORDS
WRITING PRACTICALLY
WRITING CREATIVELY
WRITING LOGICALLY
WRITING ABOUT PEOPLE

Dedicated to serving

AMSCO

our nation's youth

When ordering this book, please specify:
either R 105 W *or*
101 WAYS TO LEARN VOCABULARY

AMSCO SCHOOL PUBLICATIONS, INC.

315 Hudson Street   New York, N.Y. 10013

ACKNOWLEDGMENTS

Grateful acknowledgment is made to the following sources for permission to use copyrighted materials. They appear in this book on the pages indicated.

Doubleday & Company, Inc. *Page 147*. An excerpt from "The Cop and the Anthem" from *The Four Million* by O. Henry. Reprinted by permission of Doubleday & Company, Inc.

Harcourt Brace Jovanovich, Inc. *Page 125*. An excerpt from "Politics and the English Language" from *Shooting an Elephant and Other Essays* by George Orwell.

Angel Flores. *Page 120*. "Cabin-Kid," a translation by Dudley Fitts of Tristan Corbière's "Le Mousse."

Little, Brown and Co. *Page 145*. "Reflection on Ingenuity" from *Many Long Years Ago* by Ogden Nash. By permission of Little, Brown and Co. Copyright 1930 by Ogden Nash.

Saturday Review. Page 202. Four Wit-Twisters by Arthur Swan. Copyright 1967 by Saturday Review, Inc.

Time. Page 140. "Who Owns the Stars and Stripes?" reprinted by permission from TIME, The Weekly Newsmagazine. Copyright Time, Inc., 1970.

ISBN 0-87720-343-1

Printed in the United States of America

To the Student

How many times have you heard that one of the basic problems today—a problem underlying many other problems—is *communication*? Do you realize the full implications of this statement?

The basic substance of real communication is, of course, *thought*; but thought is shapeless, formless —is pure spirit. It must be given a body before it can be communicated. In short, it must be translated into words. Words are the flesh and blood, the muscles and nerves, that give shape and form to a thought, that make it possible for a thought to exist and to be shared.

Skeptical? Then try this experiment. Think about something for thirty seconds—the population explosion, football, your plans for the weekend.

Finished? Then think about your thinking. You used words, didn't you, in order to think?

Now communicate your thoughts to the person sitting next to you. Even more obviously, you need words in order to express those thoughts.

A knowledge of words, then, should be your first and major academic goal; skill in handling words should be your second, no less important goal.

How do you go about mastering words? The answer lies in yourself. You have already mastered many things: you know how to tune in a TV set; how to dance; how to make an involved telephone call; how to buy records and operate a phonograph. You may know how to clean a carburetor, or create an animated film, or build a model plane. How did you learn these things?

If you think about it, you will realize that all of the skills you have mastered have two things in common: they are important to you and they interest you.

The most simple task is impossible if it means nothing to you. The most difficult task becomes possible once you *want* to tackle it.

And that, precisely, is the purpose of this book: to make you *want* to tackle words!

Words aren't manufactured in a factory by scholars; they erupt into existence as they are needed. We adopt them from other languages; we coin them on impulse; we build them to handle new ideas. The twenty lessons in Part I will help you to see "How Words Are Made."

Words aren't orphans, either. Like humans, they have all kinds of relatives. Some are related by structure, some by association. If you think of a word as a member of a group, you will discover the "cobweb effect" whereby one word will remind you of many others, and all of them, loosely connected, will be readily available when you need them. This is the purpose of Part II, "Word Groups."

The best tools are worthless in the hands of an inept worker; and words are tools. Used well, words can do many things: they can persuade, refute, and justify. They can create and destroy. They can pave the way to understanding. But they can do all this only if they are used skillfully. Part III, "Handling Words," will give you practice in some of the more useful techniques.

"Word Wizardry," Part IV, offers many opportunities to test the information and the skills mastered in the first three units. It will also deepen your awareness of the richness and variety of the English language. As your memory is jogged and your skills are sharpened, you will find yourself enjoying the challenge each lesson presents.

Finally, as a sort of dessert, you are given in Part V a cluster of twenty word games. Word games are fun at parties and are pleasant time-fillers, but they are more: they will keep in "honed" condition your ability to recognize and manipulate words.

And don't forget Lesson 101. The "word-a-day" habit, once acquired, will be a lifelong asset, one that will pay rich dividends socially, economically, and intellectually. Like the fabled fountain of youth in Florida, it will keep you forever young and vigorous!

No part of this program is really new to you. You mastered all of these skills once before—when you were a toddler, learning to speak. You collected words in groups, you made up words, you tried handling them in different ways. You even experimented to see which words would bring the fastest reaction from your parents! All you really have to do now is to revive that early, temporarily forgotten learning pattern. Once you do so, you will find that real communication—one of the last human frontiers in an age of technology—will be within your grasp.

Joan D. Berbrich

Contents

Part I. How Words Are Made

Part II. Word Groups

Part III. Handling Words

Part IV. Word Wizardry

Part V. Word Games

Part I. *How Words Are Made*

How is a word made? Is it coined (that is, created) by one man? Sometimes. Is it a new form that grows from an old form? Sometimes. Is it "borrowed" from another language? Sometimes. Is it a combination of two other words? Sometimes. Is it an old word with a new meaning? Sometimes. Is it a word that was first a proper name? Sometimes. Is it slang that has been "promoted"? Sometimes.

Where does a word come from? From war? From science? From industry? From humor? From kindness? From cruelty? From all of these.

Every day new words come into our language. They come from many different sources and in many different ways. Knowing how they come and why they come will make words more meaningful and memorable.

1

1. BEGIN AT THE BEGINNING . . .

In the beginning was a *word*. Then someone, sometime, trying to express a new thought, placed a syllable in front of the old word. So the prefix was born . . . and a new word. The word *marine*, for example, refers to the ocean, or sea. When man first imagined a ship that would travel under the water, he turned naturally to the prefix that means "under"—that is, *sub*. And now *submarine* is an accepted word in our language.

A prefix is a handy tool. It has many uses. It can help you to recognize an unfamiliar word; it can help you to form the exact word you are looking for; it can help you become a sophisticated user of words by making you more aware of word relationships.

I. Let's begin with a prefix already mentioned—*sub*, meaning "under." Try to define the following words. Use a dictionary if you like, but be sure to emphasize the way the prefix affects the meaning.

*Example: sub*marine—a ship that operates *under* water

1. *sub*way _____ *Under way* _____
2. *sub*contract _____
3. *sub*scribe _____ *to write under* _____
4. *sub*standard _____ *below or understanding* _____
5. *sub*mit _____ *to put under* _____
6. *sub*soil _____
7. *sub*terranean _____ *under ground* _____
8. *sub*jugate _____ *to place under* _____
9. *sub*cutaneous _____
10. *sub*liminal _____

Note that the meaning of a prefix can change slightly; "sub" sometimes means "secondary," rather than "under." Keeping this in mind, define the following:

11. *sub*committee _____
12. *sub*station _____
13. *sub*stitute _____
14. *sub*plot _____
15. *sub*treasury _____

Finally remember that a prefix may change its spelling in adapting to the spelling of a root. Hence, before "p" *sub* becomes *sup*: suppose, supplant, suppress; before "g" *sub* becomes *sug*: suggest; before "f" *sub* becomes *suf*: suffer.

101 Ways to Learn Vocabulary

II. Here's a kind of "educated" guessing game, dealing with prefixes, that you will enjoy.

First chance: The prefix *super* means "above" or "over" or "beyond" or "greater than." How many of these "super" words can you identify?

Example: a man with greater than normal powers
Answer: superman

supernatural 1. beyond what is natural

supermarket 2. a large self-service food store

super visor 3. one who oversees or directs work or employees

supersonic 4. faster than the speed of sound

superfluous 5. above what is sufficient or required

Second chance: This time the prefix is *trans*, meaning "across" or "over" or "beyond" or "through."

transatlantic 6. across the Atlantic Ocean

transmit 7. to send across, from one person or place to another

transportation 8. the process of carrying people from one place to another

transplant 9. to remove and plant in another place

transom 10. a window above a door or another window

Third chance: Now the prefix is *circum*, meaning "around" or "about" or "on all sides."

Circumnavigate 11. to go completely around, especially by water

Circumference 12. the perimeter of a circle

Circumscribe 13. to draw a line around; to limit

Circumspect 14. cautious; inclined to look around before acting

_____ 15. to get around by deception or stratagem

III. Here is a paragraph in which fourteen words with a common prefix are used, but omitted. Each of the missing words is followed by a definition in parentheses. Use your dictionary and your ingenuity to fill in the blanks correctly.

After my nephew (1) dis *turb* ed (*interrupted*) the peace that Saturday night, I threatened to (2) dis *inherit* (*exclude from right to receive money through succession*) him. His naturally (3) dis *agreeably* (*unpleasant*) (4) dis *position* (*temperament*) had often resulted in his behaving (5) dis *grace* fully (*shamefully*), but never before had I been so (6) dis_*illusion*_ed (*disenchanted*). Even as a child, he had been (7) dis_*obedient*_ (*refractory*), but I had (8) dis_*pensed*_ed (*dealt out*) mercy rather than justice. As he grew older, the (9) dis_*pute*_s (*arguments*) between us grew in number. I tried to believe that the (10) dis_*parity*_ (*inequality or difference*) in our ages led to this constant (11) dis_*cord*_ (*lack of harmony*), but when he tormented the cat on Main Street that night, I (12) dis_*owned*_ed (*repudiated*) him. His thoroughly (13) dis_*solute*_ (*licentious*) nature could have free rein. I had (14) dis_*solved*_ed (*terminated*) our relationship.

2. . . . AND END AT THE ENDING

Just as *prefixes* precede words, forming new words, so *suffixes* follow words, forming new words. Suffixes can be almost as helpful as prefixes in helping you to recognize words and develop language awareness.

I. Let's start with an easy suffix—*-less*. It means "without." If we say that a well is bottom*less*, we mean that it literally has *no* bottom, or is *without* a bottom. How many "-less" words can you provide for the following definitions?

-------------------------------------- 1. without timidity

-------------------------------------- 2. in despair

-------------------------------------- 3. without a maternal parent

-------------------------------------- 4. without movement

-------------------------------------- 5. never becoming weary

-------------------------------------- 6. poker-faced

-------------------------------------- 7. without any money at all

-------------------------------------- 8. innumerable

-Ette (*-etta*) is a versatile suffix. Sometimes it means "little":

9. A little kitchen is a _____ .

10. A little statue is a _____ .

11. A little room is a _____ .

12. A small dining area is a _____ .

13. A little opera is an _____ .

Occasionally *-ette* indicates feminine gender:

14. A girl who leads a marching band or drum corps is a _____ .

15. A woman who fights for the vote is a _____ .

16. A woman who works on a farm is a _____ .

And occasionally *-ette* becomes simply *-et*:

17. A little island is an _____ .

18. A small flower is a _____ .

Another versatile suffix is *-age*. Sometimes it means the "act of":

19. The act of passing from one place to another is _____ .

20. The act of marrying is _____ .

21. The act of carrying is _____ .

Sometimes *-age* means a place of abode—a place where someone lives:

22. Children without parents may live in an _____ .

23. A recluse may live in a _____ .

24. Certain ecclesiastics live in a _____ .

   At other times *-age* means "amount of" or "total of":

25. The total distance a car has traveled is its _____ .

26. The total covering of feathers on a bird is its _____ .

27. The amount something may decrease (after laundering, for example) is _____ .

   Finally, the suffix *-ess* usually turns a masculine noun into a feminine noun:

28. The daughter of a king is a _____ .

29. A woman who owns a store is a _____ .

30. A woman who practices witchcraft is a _____ .

II. This time start with a word root, *port*, meaning "carry." Below is a list of suffixes. Combine *port* with one suffix to form the word that will complete each of the blanks below. (Use each suffix only once.)

   -age   -manteau   -er   -able   -folio

   A (1)_____ (type of hotel employee) offered to pick up my (2)_____ (large suitcase) and my (3)_____ (case for papers and documents). Later, when I arrived at the river, (4)_____ (the labor of carrying) of these same objects was easy because they were (5)_____ (capable of being carried).

   The second word root is *part*, meaning "a fraction of a whole." Fill each blank with *part* + an appropriate suffix.

   Because I was interested in the new splinter group, I studied carefully the (6)_____ _____ (individual items) listed in their campaign literature. A (7)_____ (sharer) I could be; a (8)_____ (devoted follower) I could not. (9)_____ (Biased) though I was toward the rebels and their ideas, I could not, at this critical time, wholly support a (10)_____ (dividing, sectioning) of the party.

3. ROOT RECOGNITION

A root, says the dictionary, is the essential part of something. A word root is the essential part of a word. Prefixes and suffixes are additions; without the root, they would have little meaning. One word root can often lead you to a knowledge of ten or twenty related words. Indeed, the word root is a key—a key to a growing vocabulary.

I. One valuable word root is *duc* (also *duce, duct*), which means to "lead." If we add the prefix *de*, we get the word *deduce* or *deduct*. If we then add the suffix *tion*, we get *deduction*. From the boxes below, choose prefixes and/or suffixes to combine with *duc* (*duce, duct*) to satisfy the following definitions.

PREFIXES		SUFFIXES
con-	re-	-ile
de-	se-	-ive
in-	tra-	-or
pro-		

-     1. an official in charge of a bus or train

-     2. creative, fruitful

-     3. to entice away, to corrupt

-     4. an adjective that describes reasoning from a general statement to an individual case

-     5. an adjective that describes reasoning from a number of individual cases to a general principle

-     6. capable of being molded or shaped

-     7. to bring down to a smaller size

-     8. to introduce; to take into military service

-     9. contributive; helpful

- 10. to speak evil of; to slander

II. This time your word root is *dic* or *dict*, meaning "say." Again, combine the word root with prefixes and/or suffixes to form words that satisfy the following definitions:

PREFIXES	SUFFIXES
ab-, ad-	-ary, -ory
bene-	-ate
contra-	-ion, -tion
in-	-(o)graph
pre-	-ment
vale-	

_____ 1. to deny directly

_____ 2. the act of blessing

_____ 3. to renounce or give up claim to a throne

_____ 4. a book of words and their meanings

_____ 5. one who has given himself up to a habit or practice

_____ 6. a recording device, especially used in business

_____ 7. a graduation speech

_____ 8. a foretelling; a prophecy

_____ 9. a formal accusation in law

_____ 10. choice of words in speaking or writing

III. The word root now is *scrib* or *scrip*, meaning "write." This time instead of definitions, there are sentences for you to complete by combining the root word with any prefixes and suffixes.

1. The doctor _____ a new drug for the complaining patient.

2. He _____ to four scientific magazines at the present time.

3. Can you give a detailed _____ of the escaped convict?

4. The child _____ all over my carefully typed term paper.

5. The film producer read the _____ and decided to buy it.

6. The secretary had to _____ her notes before she was able to leave the office.

7. After the woman's death, the legislature _____ the use of certain drugs.

8. I asked for a _____ for successful writing; I should have known better.

9. The author's personal _____ makes that copy of the book very valuable.

10. The D.A. asked for a _____ of the testimony of the key witness.

IV. The last word root is *pon* (*pone, pos, pose*), meaning "place." Combine the word root with any prefixes or suffixes to form words to complete the following sentences:

1. He wished to _____ his dental appointment until after the examination.

2. His _____ in the debate, a brilliant lawyer, was more than a match for him.

3. The nobles _____ the king, but were uncertain as to whom they should put in his place.

4. If your _____ is well written, it will be entered in the essay contest.

5. People who _____ on their friends soon have no friends.

6. His poor _____ led me to believe that he was self-conscious about being so tall.

7. When she was calm and her face was in _____, she looked younger and happier.

8. While the professors were discussing German philosophy, the rebellious student _____ a remark about unfair school regulations.

9. If one _____ one photograph on another, the result can be fascinating.

10. To everyone's astonishment, he rose to _____ a toast to his archenemy.

4. TELESCOPING WORDS

As modern life quickens in tempo, everything that is part of life (including language) is influenced by the desire for speed and short-cuts. This is especially true in America where speed has become a kind of demigod. We are always looking for a way to "save time." This explains the popularity of the sandwich (the original Earl of Sandwich must have been an American by nature!) and of the short story (which can be read quickly between two other tasks). This attitude also explains the growing popularity of telescoped words. Why use two tools when one will do? Why use two words when one will do?

Use your American ingenuity to combine the two underlined words in each of the following sentences to form a new "telescoped" word.

Example: If you get up too late for breakfast and too early for lunch, you may settle for _ _ _ _ _ _ .
Answer: brunch (*br* from breakfast, *unch* from lunch)

1. If you are driving and you wish to stop at a hotel that caters to motorists, you will be looking for

    a _ _ _ _ _ _ _ _ _ _ _ _ .

2. If the state decides to execute a criminal with the aid of electricity, it _ _ _ _ _ _ _ _ _ _ _ _ _ _ _ _ _ him.

3. If an industrial city is plagued by smoke and by fog, the residents suffer from the irritating, un-

    healthful man-made phenomenon known as _ _ _ _ _ _ _ _ _ _ .

4. If a person is addicted to the cinema, he may be called a _ .

5. If you are dreaming up daffy definitions for a local newspaper, you will probably call your column

    _ .

6. The astronaut has a special tool that can be used both as pliers and wrench; it is called, logically,

    a _ _ _ _ _ _ _ _ _ _ _ _ _ _ _ .

7. He has a second tool, a space hammer, which is known as a _ _ _ _ _ _ _ _ _ _ _ _ _ _ _ _ _ .

8. A Southerner who remains loyal to the traditions of Dixie but who also considers himself a Democrat

    is known as a _ .

9. The science of aviation electronics recently became known as _ _ _ _ _ _ _ _ _ _ _ _ _ _ _ _ _ .

10. A marathon on television, usually produced for a charitable organization, is called a _ _ _ _ _ _ _ _ _ _ _ _ .

11. A barbecue for melting junked cars is rather facetiously called a _ _ _ _ _ _ _ _ _ _ _ _ _ _ _ _ _ .

12. A verb that describes the lifting of military personnel to a new location by helicopter is

    _ _ _ _ _ _ _ _ _ _ _ _ _ _ _ _ .

13. A telegram sent by cable is a _ .

14. News that is broadcasted is called a _ _ _ _ _ _ _ _ _ _ _ _ _ _ _ _ _ .

15. _ _ _ _ _ _ _ _ _ _ _ _ _ _ _ provides medical care for the aged.

5. ACRONYMS

An *acronym* is a word formed from the initial letters of other words. The reason for forming an acronym is obvious: to substitute a short, easily remembered word for a long or cumbersome title. Most acronyms are formed *after* the title has been determined; occasionally an acronym is chosen before a title is developed to fit it. The latter is probably true of WAVES and CARE.

I. Below are ten commonly used acronyms. For how many of them can you provide the full title?

Example: WASP
Answer: *W*omen's *A*ir Force *S*ervice *P*ilots

1. WAC   --
2. AWOL   --
3. DECA   --
4. RADAR   --
5. NATO   --
6. SeaBees   --
7. ZIP   --
8. WITCH   --
9. CARE   --
10. NOW   --

II. Now try the reverse procedure. Below are ten titles from which acronyms have been made. How many can you identify?

Example: Women's Royal Naval Service
Answer: WRENS

- -------------- 1. light amplification by stimulated emission of radiation
- -------------- 2. Youth International Party
- -------------- 3. Congress of Racial Equality
- -------------- 4. Volunteers in Service to America
- -------------- 5. Fabbrica Italiano Automobile Torino
- -------------- 6. United Nations Educational, Scientific and Cultural Organization
- -------------- 7. Standard Oil Company of New York
- -------------- 8. self-contained underwater breathing apparatus
- -------------- 9. situation normal, all fouled up
- -------------- 10. long-range navigation

6. ALPHABET SOUP

One result of our native love for speed and short-cuts is the "alphabet soup" apparent in any daily newspaper or magazine. "Alphabet soup" refers to those abbreviations that become so popular that everyone knows what they mean although many people have forgotten the words that the initials literally represent. Have you?

If you haven't, you will be able to "translate" the following paragraphs. Just write in the meaning of each abbreviation, and the paragraph will immediately make sense (if it doesn't already!).

I. When the G.P. (1)_____ (who had been detained at a PTA (2)_____ meeting) arrived, he was met by an anxious R.N. (3)_____ . On the QT (4)_____ she asked him if her patient, a VIP (5)_____ , had TB (6)_____ . "The CIA (7)_____ and the FBI (8)_____ are both interested in him," she said. "He has an extraordinary I.Q. (9)_____ ." "All he needs," the G.P. said reassuringly, "is TLC (10)_____ ."

II. The GOP (1)_____ gave a dance for the DAR (2)_____ . The invitations were marked R.S.V.P. (3)_____ . On the night of the dance, the director of the FHA (4)_____ came; so did the director of the FCC (5)_____ . It was covered by NBC (6)_____ , by CBS (7)_____ , and by ABC (8)_____ . At six p.m. (9)_____ the food that had been ordered arrived C.O.D. (10)_____ .

III. The D.A. (1)_____ and the C.P.A. (2)_____ started for the theater. They were delayed by some MP's (3)_____ who had had a telephone call about them from the SPCA (4)_____ . Was it true they were carrying

TNT (5)_____? It was a mistake, everyone soon realized, and they were released. But the play they wanted to see was S.R.O. (6)_____ _____, so they headed for their homes, instead, for a viewing of the championship fight on TV (7)_____. "With a little ESP (8)_____ _____, we could have avoided the delay," said the C.P.A. "Oh, well," replied the D.A., "just so long as we get home before the k.o. (9)_____." P.S. (10)___ _____: They did.

IV. Fill in the blanks. Then answer these questions—if you can!

1. Why is TGIF _____ a favorite expression among teachers?

_____

_____

2. How does an M.O. _____ help to capture a criminal?

_____

_____

3. Why are the letters R.I.P. _____ often engraved on tombstones?

_____

_____

4. What year A.D. _____ is this?   _____

5. Why is CATV _____ an exciting development?

_____

_____

7. AMERICANISMS

Many of our most vivid words are Americanisms, coined for a specific purpose. These include standard, colloquial, and slang expressions. See how many you can identify from the clues given. The number of blanks corresponds to the number of letters in the word.

____ ____   1. a car that "burns up" the road

____ _____   2. absolutely confidential

_____-_____   3. to park a car alongside another

_____ _____   4. a melodramatic afternoon TV show

_____   5. traveling by securing free rides in passing vehicles

____ ____   6. a picnic favorite, especially with sauerkraut, mustard, catsup, or relish

_____   7. a mystery story

_____-___   8. a theater where patrons can remain in their automobiles

_____   9. a large self-service food store

____   10. a celebrity (abbr.)

_____-_____   11. a necessary adjunct for the parents' night out

_____-_____   12. a prospector

_____   13. lots of snow, plus wind

_____   14. boys and girls in school together

_____   15. a chum, a pal

_____   16. more formal than a kitchen nook, less formal than a dining room

_____-_____ ____   17. salary that is left *after* taxes and other deductions

_____ _____   18. one who serves at an ice cream fountain

_____   19. a restaurant without waiters

____ _____   20. a place where automobiles are cleaned

Here's another group of Americanisms. These deal, directly or indirectly, with the making and accumulation of money.

_____   21. a premium given to promote sales

_____   22. an advertisement given away on streets or slipped under doors

____ _____   23. an idea or "lode" that promises to be extremely fruitful

____ _____   24. the rapid, intensive, competitive activity we all engage in

_____ _____   25. someone who is over-enthusiastic, especially at work

_____   26. constructed beforehand

_____-____   27. one who *always* agrees with his superior

_____—_____   28. to inspect examples of work done, at random

This group comes from our historical past.

_____ _____   29. area subject to dust storms

_____   30. to use long speeches to prevent a legislature from voting

_____-   31. one who makes a career slipping through ships stationed in a
_____   harbor to prevent entry or departure

_____   32. arbitrary arrangement of political divisions to give one party
                           an unfair advantage

Some deal with our social attitudes and our personality.

_____   33. a pedestrian who disregards traffic directions in crossing the
                           street

_____   34. a person of intellectual tastes

_____   35. a person of uncultivated tastes

_____   36. an intellectual (colloquial; often meant disparagingly)

_____   37. a tendency in some mothers to dominate society, in general,
                           and their sons, in particular

And some deal with our leisure activities.

_____   38. an iced drink of alcoholic liquors mixed with flavoring in-
                           gredients

_____   39. an attendant who takes orders and serves food to customers in
                           automobiles

_____   40. ice cream served with fruit or syrup

8. OUR ENGLISH COUSINS

American English is sometimes considered a separate language, but our ties to British English are close and enduring. Most of the time we and our English cousins understand each other. We enjoy British movies, and they delight in American TV. Only occasionally is our enjoyment ruffled by the unfamiliar word or by the word that sounds familiar but seems inappropriate in context. You probably are acquainted with Carnaby Street, with Piccadilly Circus, and with other place-names in London, but how well do you really know British English?

I. To find out, try to translate the following British English into American English.

The Short Odyssey of Peter Sayers

Peter Sayers made a last-minute check before he left his *flat* _____ _____. With a new *vest* _____ and new *braces* _____ , he felt ready for anything. As the *lift* _____ squeaked its way downward, Peter wondered if Millie would like to go to the *flickers* _____ that night. Outside he carefully skirted the *dustbin* _____ and headed for the *chemist's* _____. Just next to the chemist's was the City Bank, and as Peter approached, two *bank raiders* _____ dashed out of the bank and into a parked *lorry* _____. After the first shock subsided, Peter decided he must act as a good citizen. He entered a *call box* _____ and dialed Scotland Yard. A few minutes later he emerged satisfied, knowing that the matter was in good hands.

(A score of 9–10 indicates true international aplomb. 7–8: After a few more James Bond mysteries, you'll be ready for a trip to England. 5–6: You're a good neighbor, but that's about all. Under 5: You had better spend another few years watching British flickers!)

II. Without seeing the words in context, can you give the American equivalent for each of the following British terms?

1. biscuit _____
2. black treacle _____
3. bonnet _____
4. minerals _____
5. hood _____
6. parking pitch _____
7. dustman _____

8. boots   ----------------------------------

9. boarding   ----------------------------------

10. draughts   ----------------------------------

11. scones   ----------------------------------

12. multiple shop   ----------------------------------

13. post   ----------------------------------

14. petrol   ----------------------------------

15. sleeping partner   ----------------------------------

III. This time give the British equivalent for each of the following American terms:

1. garters   --------------------------------

2. baby carriage   --------------------------------

3. corn   --------------------------------

4. cigar store   --------------------------------

5. peanuts   --------------------------------

6. can (container)   --------------------------------

7. bumper (of a car)   --------------------------------

8. flashlight   --------------------------------

9. grade (in school)   --------------------------------

10. overcoat   --------------------------------

11. policeman   --------------------------------

12. radio   --------------------------------

13. trolley   --------------------------------

14. dessert   --------------------------------

15. subway   --------------------------------

9. EITHER A BORROWER OR A LENDER BE!

When Shakespeare wrote "Neither a borrower, nor a lender be," he was referring to money, not language. For borrowing and lending are essential if a language is to be constantly updated and exact. This is especially true in today's world where mass media and international trade provide interests and products common to all nations.

Because this is true, *loanwords* exist. A *loanword*, according to *The American Heritage Dictionary*, is "a word adopted from another language that has become at least partly naturalized." If the spelling and pronunciation have changed or if the word has become exceedingly popular, we may forget that it is a loanword that started life in another language. Who today remembers that "sherbet" is Turkish, or that "discotheque" is French? Yet realizing that many of our English words are loanwords is important. Such a realization can give us added insight into ourselves and into the nations from which we borrow. And the loanwords themselves make our daily language richer, more colorful, and more exciting than it would otherwise be.

Below are definitions of loanwords listed by country of origin. As you work with each group, note the characteristics of that group: the sound of the words, the letter combinations, the subject matter. This will give you some insight into the characteristics of other nations that we in this country tend to emphasize.

French

---------------------- 1. a chest of drawers, usually with a mirror; also a government department

---------------------- 2. a tract of level land covered by coarse grass without trees

---------------------- 3. a building for housing automobiles

---------------------- 4. a dish made of fish, crackers, onions, etc., stewed together, often in milk

---------------------- 5. of little value; petty; mean

---------------------- 6. a vixenish woman; a hag

---------------------- 7. a flourish of trumpets; a showy display

---------------------- 8. awkward; tactless

German

---------------------- 9. a school for children younger than six

---------------------- 10. cabbage cut and fermented in brine

---------------------- 11. a sudden, overpowering attack, usually accompanied by bombing

---------------------- 12. a toasted biscuit or rusk

---------------------- 13. a sweet cake cut in strips and fried brown in deep fat

---------------------- 14. prepared foods; also a store in which such foods are sold

-------------------------------- 15. a strong desire to ramble, or travel without a set course

Italian

-------------------------------- 16. with one's identity concealed; masked

-------------------------------- 17. one who follows an art as a pastime; an amateur

-------------------------------- 18. a platform, enclosed by a railing, projecting from the outer wall of a building

-------------------------------- 19. a ludicrous and total failure

-------------------------------- 20. a spectacular show with an elaborate setting

-------------------------------- 21. a cave; a place of retreat

-------------------------------- 22. bizarre; distorted; absurdly incongruous

Spanish

-------------------------------- 23. a very large lizard, like a crocodile, with a short, broad snout

-------------------------------- 24. an enclosure for confining animals

-------------------------------- 25. a whirling, destructive wind, accompanied by a funnel-shaped cloud

-------------------------------- 26. a flat-topped hill with steeply sloping sides

-------------------------------- 27. a structure made of unburnt bricks

-------------------------------- 28. unexpected good fortune

-------------------------------- 29. a courtyard; an open porch

Japanese

-------------------------------- 30. an industrial magnate

-------------------------------- 31. self-defense without weapons

-------------------------------- 32. a Japanese singing and dancing girl

-------------------------------- 33. a loose robe, tied with a sash

-------------------------------- 34. a legume, or seed, that yields oil, flour, meal

Dutch

-------------------------------- 35. a salad made of chopped cabbage

-------------------------------- 36. a small covered porch at a house door; the steps leading to the door

---------------------------- 37. a vehicle on runners, used for carrying people over snow

---------------------------- 38. a small, thin, flat cake

---------------------------- 39. a foreman; a manager

Irish

---------------------------- 40. a female spirit whose wailings foretell death

---------------------------- 41. in abundance; plentifully

---------------------------- 42. a ruffian, or hoodlum

---------------------------- 43. a small fairy, often a tricky old man, who if caught may reveal hidden treasure

Scandinavian

---------------------------- 44. to glide on strips of wood bound to the feet

---------------------------- 45. a soft but crisp indented cake of batter cooked in a special iron

---------------------------- 46. a meal of appetizers served buffet style

Arabic

---------------------------- 47. an imaginary evil being who robs graves and feeds on corpses

---------------------------- 48. civilian dress, when worn by a military officer

---------------------------- 49. a kind of hemp chewed or smoked for its intoxicating effect

Portuguese

---------------------------- 50. a large parrot with brilliant plumage

Russian

---------------------------- 51. a kind of whip for flogging criminals

---------------------------- 52. a wolfhound, known for grace and swiftness

Turkish

---------------------------- 53. a crowd, or pack, or swarm

---------------------------- 54. empty talk; nonsense

Australian

--------------------------- 55. a curved club that, when thrown, returns to its user

--------------------------- 56. a marsupial mammal with a small head and powerful hind legs

Hungarian

--------------------------- 57. a ragout of beef or veal

Yiddish

--------------------------- 58. a meddler; one who gives gratuitous advice

Hindu

--------------------------- 59. a one-story building, often with a wide veranda

South Pacific

--------------------------- 60. forbidden by tradition or social usage

10. OUR POLYGLOT CITIZENRY

Americans have a reputation for language-laziness; we expect "foreigners" to speak English, preferably American English, wherever we travel. But in self-defense we should point out that we have been exceedingly liberal in adopting words and phrases from all over the world. Words taken from another language and Anglicized, or words influenced by another language, were discussed in the last chapter; but here are other words and phrases, retaining their original spelling and pronunciation, that every educated English-speaking person should know. You may, without realizing it, be speaking several languages daily!

Try matching these definitions and phrases to see how good a linguist you are.

I. From Latin:

____	1. modus operandi	*a.*	with praise
____	2. ante bellum	*b.*	in good faith; genuine
____	3. cum laude	*c.*	privately, confidentially
____	4. persona non grata	*d.*	before the war (especially the Civil War)
____	5. sine qua non	*e.*	without limit
____	6. sub rosa	*f.*	time flies
____	7. status quo	*g.*	a person not acceptable
____	8. ad infinitum	*h.*	a method of operating, especially with reference to criminals
____	9. bona fide	*i.*	the existing state of affairs
____	10. tempus fugit	*j.*	the necessary thing

From Latin:

____	11. non sequitur	*a.*	the characters in a play
____	12. ad hoc	*b.*	my fault, my guilt
____	13. ex post facto	*c.*	that which does not follow
____	14. in loco parentis	*d.*	by virtue of an office
____	15. mea culpa	*e.*	in the place of a parent
____	16. de facto	*f.*	with a retroactive effect
____	17. non compos mentis	*g.*	not of sound mind
____	18. alter ego	*h.*	special; for one purpose only
____	19. dramatis personae	*i.*	in fact; actually
____	20. ex officio	*j.*	a second self

101 Ways to Learn Vocabulary

II. From **French**:

----	1. pièce de résistance	*a.* having a harmonious relationship
----	2. au revoir	*b.* a decisive finishing stroke
----	3. raison d'être	*c.* the best; the chief piece of a collection
----	4. esprit de corps	*d.* an understanding; an agreement
----	5. coup d'état	*e.* justification for existence
----	6. carte blanche	*f.* a false step; an offense against social convention
----	7. en rapport	*g.* unconditional power (blank check)
----	8. coup de grâce	*h.* group spirit and enthusiasm
----	9. entente	*i.* good-bye; till we meet again
----	10. faux pas	*j.* unexpected political move

From **French**:

----	11. fin de siècle	*a.* knowing how to do or say the right thing
----	12. bête noire	*b.* a person or object feared or hated
----	13. fait accompli	*c.* an author's pen name
----	14. laissez-faire	*d.* a fixed idea; an obsession
----	15. savoir faire	*e.* end of the century; especially characteristic of the end of the nineteenth century
----	16. nom de plume	*f.* pleasant trip
----	17. bon voyage	*g.* noninterference by the government
----	18. avant-garde	*h.* the vanguard; the leaders (sometimes, the extremists)
----	19. cause célèbre	*i.* a thing accomplished, presumably irrevocable
----	20. idée fixe	*j.* a celebrated legal case; a legal case that appeals to the popular imagination and that establishes a new precedent

III. From **German**:

----	1. ersatz	*a.* a group for coffee and gossip
----	2. kaput	*b.* substituted for the real thing
----	3. leitmotif	*c.* anxiety, fear
----	4. kaffee klatsch	*d.* smashed; ruined; finished
----	5. angst	*e.* a theme that runs throughout a musical or literary work

IV. From Japanese:

____	1. karate	*a.*	a form of Japanese Buddhism
____	2. sukiyaki	*b.*	a member of the military class
____	3. Zen	*c.*	a dish prepared from meat and vegetables
____	4. samurai	*d.*	a method of defending oneself without the use of weapons
____	5. haiku	*e.*	a 3-line, 17-syllable poem, usually imagistic or mood-portraying; unrhymed

V. From Yiddish:

____	1. kosher	*a.*	a sentimental or florid quality in music, art, or literature
____	2. kibitzer	*b.*	a hard doughnut-shaped roll
____	3. schlemiel	*c.*	a giver of unwanted advice
____	4. schmaltz	*d.*	lawful, proper
____	5. bagel	*e.*	an unlucky person for whom nothing ever goes right

VI. From Greek:

____	1. acme	*a.*	glory, renown
____	2. apotheosis	*b.*	an exclamation of triumph at a discovery
____	3. alpha	*c.*	the highest point; peak
____	4. eureka	*d.*	deification of a person
____	5. kudos	*e.*	the letter A; hence, the beginning

11. STORY-WORDS

One is never too young or too old to enjoy a story. So this is storytime—a chance to relax, read a few stories, and guess the "missing" words.

1. During the great European plagues, bodies of the dead were piled in great heaps and burned, mainly to prevent further spread of the dreaded disease. Today we use the fires to get rid of leaves or wood instead of bodies. The word is _____.

2. In central Europe a long time ago the favorite bearer of burdens was the donkey, or ass (*esel*, in German). A traveler could pile his belongings on one as he set forth on a long journey. A peddler, wandering from town to town, could transport his wares on one. Then, in the seventeenth century, artists contrived a wooden frame that would support a picture while it was being painted or displayed. The name chosen for this supporting structure was, naturally enough, a(n) _____.

3. According to one story, in the sixteenth century, children who studied hard and learned their prayers were rewarded by being given little twisted cakes. The twists may have represented the folded arms of the religious teachers. The Latin word for a small reward is "pretiola." The word today for these little twisted cakes is _____.

4. In ancient Athens if citizens wished to banish a man, they voted against him by placing his name on a piece of clay or shell, called an "ostrakon." If 6,000 citizens so voted, the man was forced to leave the city. Today we simply exclude someone from our own society. The word is _____.

5. In eleventh-century Persia a group of hashish-eaters organized to destroy Christian leaders. These hashish-eaters were called *hashshashin* in Arabic. Today anyone who kills someone very important, especially a government leader, is called a(n) _____.

6. John _____ Scotus was a thirteenth-century philosopher and theologian. This quite brilliant man gained many adherents who were called _____ men. For a while they were highly respected, but within a couple of centuries new ideas were being proposed. When these followers refused to follow the new ideas, the word _____ men became a derisive epithet. It was soon shortened to _____ and now suggests stupidity—especially in the classroom!

7. This word, in French, originally meant "stuffing." Later, a short comedy was "stuffed" between two serious plays. Soon the short comedy was being called a(n) _____. Today it refers to a comic play or any absurdly comic act.

8. This word once named a weapon: a rotating beam with large spikes, used mainly against men on horseback. Its shape eventually led to its being used as a kind of turnstile at one end of a road and then as part of a tollgate. Soon any road having a tollgate was called a(n)_____. Now the name applies to almost any highway.

9. During the feudal period serfs had to grind their grain at the mill belonging to their lord. These mills were called *bannal* mills—meaning "common to all." Today, we call a word used by everyone all the time trite, or _ _ _ _ _ _ _ _ _ _ _ _ .

10. In Italian cities in the later Middle Ages, pawnbroking—lending money on articles left as security—was a popular trade. Most pawnbrokers soon collected many odds and ends, including old furniture. As this "junk" piled up, it became known as _ _ _ _ _ _ _ _ _ _ _ , because the Lombards were among the leading pawnbrokers. Today, a pile of timber sawn into rough planks also is called _ _ _ _ _ _ _ _ _ _ , perhaps because it resembles slightly the old furniture of the Lombards.

Many other words have fascinating stories. If you are interested, look up some of these:

curfew	goblin	intoxicate
maudlin	vogue	tantalize
bloomers	coconut	debonair
valentine	broker	focus
quarantine	muscle	police
ignoramus	derrick	bizarre
jinx	mesmerize	bedlam
thimble	swindler	daisy

Below is a partial bibliography which will help you to find the origin and history of many of these words.

Any unabridged dictionary, especially the *Oxford English Dictionary*
Shipley, Joseph: *Dictionary of Word Origins*, Philosophical Library, 1945
Garrison, Webb: *Why You Say It*, Abingdon Press, 1955
Brewer, E. C., ed.: *Dictionary of Phrase and Fable*, Harper and Brothers, 1953
Brewer, E. C., ed.: *The Reader's Handbook*, J. B. Lippincott, 1904
Weekley, Ernest: *The Romance of Words*, E. P. Dutton, 1914
Severn, William: *People Words*, Ives Washburn, 1966
Asimov, Isaac: *Words From History*, Houghton Mifflin, 1968
Encyclopaedia Britannica
Encyclopedia Americana

12. COMPOUND CARNIVAL

Compound words are unusually graphic. They often come into existence by popular demand. They are formed simply by combining two words that are in current usage.

There are three kinds of compound words:

1. Solid: two words written as one word

   Examples: spacecraft, hardtop

2. Hyphenated: two words separated by a hyphen

   Examples: sit-in, freeze-dry

3. Phrase: a word comprising two distinct words

   Examples: cold war, free flight

Notice that many compound words are of recent origin. Today so many new products are appearing on the market, so many new concepts being developed, that the people in charge automatically look for words already familiar and therefore easy to remember.

The highway constructed for speed in long-distance driving has been in existence for only a couple of decades—yet already several compound words have been coined for them: superhighway, thruway (or throughway), and freeway.

Compounding is one of the most often-used techniques for coining new words. Try your skill at "creating" compound words that solve the following "equations."

    Example: a building used for teaching and learning + a male child = a would-be scholar
    Answer: school + boy = schoolboy

1. an asterisk + to stare = to daydream

   ------------ + ------------ = -------------------------

2. an equine + a guffaw = a boisterous sound of enjoyment

   ------------ + ------------ = -------------------------

3. a sphere + a sharp end = a type of pen

   ------------ + ------------ = -------------------------

4. a facet + a promenade = a pavement for pedestrians

   ------------ + ------------ = -------------------------

5. a volume + a soft-bodied invertebrate = a studious person

   ------------ + ------------ = -------------------------

6. to murder + gladness = one who spoils fun for everyone

   ------------ + ------------ = -------------------------

7. a very young person + a head covering = a time of one's life

   ------------ + ------------ = -------------------------

8. a cut or notch + an appellation = a familiar cognomen

 ------------ + ------------ = ------------------------

9. an instrument used in working + a rude structure = a home for lathes and drills

 ------------ + ------------ = ------------------------

10. a fruit + a liquid relish = nonsense (colloquial)

 ------------ + ------------ = ------------------------

11. a pulpy fruit + a trailing plant = a relay system for gossip (colloquial)

 ------------ + ------------ = ------------------------

12. something to be chewed + a foot covering = a detective (slang)

 ------------ + ------------ = ------------------------

13. coconut liquid + a bribe = an unmanly fellow

 ------------ + ------------ = ------------------------

14. intermediate + interval of darkness = the witching hour

 ------------ + ------------ = ------------------------

15. a lump of earth + a leaper = a clumsy boor

 ------------ + ------------ = ------------------------

16. a feline + Pisces = a bullhead

 ------------ + ------------ = ------------------------

17. a watchman + a residence = a military jail

 ------------ + ------------ = ------------------------

18. filth + an implement with tines = to expose in print (colloquial)

 ------------ + ------------ = ------------------------

19. metal band + a director = an instigator of a rebellion

 ------------ + ------------ = ------------------------

20. a drama + the hinder part = the act of checking the reproduction of a recording

 ------------ + ------------ = ------------------------

13. A WORD IS A WORD, BUT . . . .

"A rose is a rose is a rose," said Gertrude Stein, and a word is a word is a word. But the rose may be red, white, peach, or a hundred other shades, and the word may sometimes mean a dozen different things. Only in context can we understand the exact meaning of many words.

Begin with a common word like *run*. What does *run* mean . . .

to a girl? (a run in her stocking)
to a track star? (fast movement)
to a financier? (a run on the banks)
to a political candidate? (to run for office)
to a sailor? (to run aground)
to a painter? (one color running into another)
to a machinist? (to run a machine)
to an actor? (Will the play have a long run?)
to a smuggler? (to run the blockade)
to a gambler? (a run of luck)
to a grocer? (a run on coffee)
to a traveler? (to take a run up to Montreal)
to a fisherman? (a run of fish upstream)
to a baseball player? (a home run)
to a freedom-loving child? (to have the run of the house)

There are about eighty other possible ways to use the word *run*, but these should suffice to emphasize the importance of context.

I. Now try it with the word *take*. What does it mean . . .

_____ 1. to a hungry person?

_____ 2. to a mathematician?

_____ 3. to a winner?

_____ 4. to a stenographer?

_____ 5. to a photographer?

II. Try it with the word *grace*. What does it mean . . .

_____ 1. to a debtor?

_____ 2. to a theologian?

_____ 3. to a diner?

_____ 4. to a duke?

_____ 5. to a musician?

III. Now take the word *jump*. What does it mean . . .

--   1. to a checkers player?

--   2. to a bridge player?

--   3. to one charged with a crime?

--   4. to a train engineer?

--   5. to a miner?

IV. Next take the word *charge*. What does it mean . . .

--   1. to an automobile mechanic?

--   2. to a lawyer?

--   3. to a store owner?

--   4. to a cavalry officer?

--   5. to an artilleryman?

V. Finally, take the word *block*. What does it mean . . .

--   1. to a child?

--   2. to a philatelist?

--   3. to a homeowner?

--   4. to a theater agent?

--   5. to a football player?

14. BODY-BUILDING

The human body has many, many parts, and each part is so precious, so important to us, that we have used its name for inanimate objects and for intangible concepts.

Start with a fairly simple part of the body—let's say the "heel." Now everyone knows the meaning of *heel* as part of the foot, but search your memory (and your dictionary) to discover the other meanings of *heel*:

> the heel of a shoe
> the heel of a loaf of bread
> the "heel" who is a contemptible person

Consider what the word *heel* means in each of the above uses. What popular phrases can you think of that employ the word *heel*? You should come up with some of the following:

> at one's heels
> down at the heels
> take to one's heels
> to heel a dog

Proceed next to compound words that have been formed from the word *heel*.

> heeler (in the political sense)
> heel-and-toe
> the heeling (tilting) of a ship

Now that the word *heel* has been thoroughly analyzed, try the same approach with the names of other parts of the body. You will be amazed at the versatility of words as you meet this challenge!

1. Part of the body: ARM

   a. Common expressions:

   ----

   b. Compound words:

   ----

2. Part of the body: FACE

   a. Common expressions:

   ----

b. Compound words:

----

3. Part of the body: LEG

   a. Common expressions:

   ----

   b. Compound words:

   ----

4. Part of the body: FOOT

   a. Common expressions:

   ----

   b. Compound words:

   ----

5. Part of the body: HAND

   a. Common expressions:

   ----

   b. Compound words:

   ----

101 Ways to Learn Vocabulary

6. Part of the body: HEAD

    a. Common expressions:

      ----

    b. Compound words:

      ----

7. Part of the body: HEART

    a. Common expressions:

      ----

    b. Compound words:

      ----

15. EUPHEMISMS

A euphemism is a mild or pleasant expression substituted for a harsh or disagreeable one. Euphemisms have probably been in existence as long as language has, but they have come into their own in our time.

Euphemisms are most often used to change the "image" of a particular group or occupation. Consider the difference between a *senior citizen* and an *old man* or *old woman*. What is the connotation of each term? Why is the first more popular today? The reason for euphemisms should now be obvious, and you are ready for step I.

I. Can you think of a current euphemism for each of the following terms?

1. boss _____
2. worker _____
3. undertaker _____
4. policeman _____
5. preacher _____
6. janitor _____
7. headwaiter _____
8. truant officer _____
9. tree trimmer _____
10. garbage man _____

II. Fill in the missing words.

Euphemisms are also used to soften unpleasant aspects of life. We hesitate to say, "James *died*." Instead we say, "James (1)_____ _____." The *coffin* has become the (2)_____; we are no longer *buried*, but (3)_____.

For the same reason *crazy* yielded to (4)_____, which yielded to (5)_____. And the *insane asylum* has become, of course, the (6)_____ _____.

III. Fill in the missing words.

Euphemisms come into use whenever public attention is focused on a particular problem or group—especially if the public or the minority group concerned is rather embarrassed at the situation. Note that the biological euphemism is less commonly used today than in the past. No one now says *limbs* for *legs*. But the sociological euphemism is more common than it used to be—as when we say not the *poor* but the (1)_____, or the (2)_____. This change can tell us something interesting about our own age.

IV. Can you provide the current euphemism for each of the underlined terms in the following sentences? As you do, consider *why* each euphemism came into existence at this time. You will find it an enlightening experience.

--- 1. The <u>juvenile delinquent</u> was brought before the judge.

--- 2. The college students <u>invaded and occupied</u> the Administration Building.

--- 3. The UN promised to help the <u>backward countries</u> of the world.

--- 4. Representatives of the two generations met for a <u>face-to-face exchange of ideas.</u>

--- 5. The <u>lazy</u> student failed to complete his term project.

--- 6. In the twentieth century the <u>lack of faith</u> between public officials and citizens seems to be increasing.

--- 7. After smashing windows and burning stores, the demonstrators demanded <u>that they not be punished.</u>

16. METAPHOR MAGIC

When we look at a very tall building, we feel respect for the engineering skill that made it possible. But we should feel wonder, too—and we would if we remembered the name for such a structure: *skyscraper*. Have you ever thought about the literal meaning of *skyscraper*? It suggests a building so tall that it scrapes the sky! It's a magnificent image that we use too often without appreciation.

A word like *skyscraper* is metaphorical. It is not literally true, but it is figuratively true—the building *seems* to scrape the sky. The word defines through imagination rather than through fact.

Words that are metaphorical are powerful because they appeal to the imagination and to the emotions. Sometimes the original word or name (e.g., skyscraper) is metaphorical. More often a word already part of our language is extended—given a new metaphorical meaning.

Have you ever described someone as being a *dynamo*? A *dynamo* is a generator that produces current. What you were really saying is that this person seems to create energy and power just as a dynamo does. You were speaking metaphorically.

Metaphorical extension creates a new word by doubling the meaning of an old word. So *dynamo*, in a sense, is now two words.

You know, of course, that *dynamite* is a powerful explosive. But what is meant if we say that a situation is *dynamite*?

You know that a *chisel* is a tool used to cut or chip away at wood. But what is meant if we say that someone is trying to *chisel* the government by claiming an illegal deduction on his taxes?

(Note: Slang is often metaphorical. *Chisel*, for example, is slang, usually acceptable in speech but not in writing.)

I. Now try your skill at analyzing metaphorical language. Can you answer the following questions? Take time to *enjoy* each metaphor as you analyze it!

1. Why does a teacher sometimes call a particular classroom a *playpen*?

   ----

2. How does one *cultivate* a friendship?

   ----

3. As the veterans returned after World War II, why did housing developments *mushroom*?

   ----

4. If you *screen* applicants for a position, what do you do?

   ----

5. What kind of meeting is a *summit* meeting?

   ----

6. When might a city be called a *jungle*?

    ----

7. How can opinions *crystallize*?

    ----

8. What kind of person is described as a *doormat*?

    ----

9. If you are frightened or caught doing something wrong, you may *freeze*. What do you literally do?

    ----

10. If you do not especially like school, what period in the day is an *oasis* for you?

II. Animal names often gain a metaphorical meaning. Sometimes a father will call his two-year-old son "Tiger," both as contrast and as encouragement; and everyone, at one time or another, has been a "mule," perhaps even a "jackass"! Can you insert in each blank below an animal or bird name that satisfies the definition in parentheses?

   1. The eighteen-year-old _____ed (pestered) his parents until they bought him a car.

   2. Children like to _____ (repeat without understanding) their parents.

   3. When things became difficult, he tried to _____ out (back out, sneak out) of the agreement.

   4. If he is not popular, it is understandable—he likes to _____ (take more than his share of) the whole show.

   5. No one wants to lunch with him—he _____s (eats voraciously) his food.

III. Terms used in leisure-time activities also gain metaphorical meanings. Have you ever considered why a swan dive is called a *swan* dive? Or what a friend means when he tells you sharply to *paddle your own canoe*? Write a sentence using each of the following terms metaphorically:

   1. dive (verb)

    ----

   2. pawn (noun)

    ----

   3. tackle (verb)

Part I. How Words Are Made

4. clear sailing

----

5. checkmate (verb)

By now you should be thinking metaphorically. The next time you write, be foxy: bombard your reader with metaphorical projectiles!

17. NEW IDEAS = NEW WORDS

In our twentieth century, we have seen new words come into existence to match new concepts and new discoveries. We need words to converse, even to think. Can you imagine how difficult life would be if instead of saying, "Please hand me that book," we had to say, "Please hand me that rectangular object with the hard cloth covers and the printed pages"? A fantastic number of words have come into our language in the last thirty years: World War II gave birth to some, the computer to others, and space exploration to still others.

But *how* do these new words come into existence?

I. Some are coined:

    1. _____ was coined by Norbert Weiner of M.I.T. in 1947 as a name for the science of the analysis of the operations of machines, especially computers.

    2. _____, an immense hollow "ball" containing a panorama of the future, was coined in the late 1930's for use at the New York World's Fair.

    3. _____ was coined in 1943 to name a "miracle" drug produced from molds.

II. Some come from prototypes:

    1. _____, meaning "collaborator," comes from Major Vidkun _____, who collaborated with the Germans in Norway in 1940.

    2. The _____ engine, an internal-combustion engine that burns oil instead of gasoline, was named after its inventor, Dr. Rudolf _____.

    3. _____, a day for which some momentous event is planned, originally referred to June 6, 1944, when British and American forces invaded the Continent.

III. Some grow from words or word parts already current in our language:

    1. _____ means a parade of cars.

    2. _____ means a board towed by a motorboat.

    3. _____ means a war in which arms and physical conflict are not used.

Regardless of how it originated, each word came into existence because it was *needed*. Once accepted, each new word enriches our language and facilitates our thinking and our expression.

IV. Sources of New Words

    One fruitful source of new words is war—perhaps because war comes with violence and revives primitive emotions. We found the word (1)_____ in London in 1938 when German bombers threatened, and Englishmen put out the lights or draped their windows. We found the word (2)_____ in 1940 when German bombs, death-carrying and lightning-fast, tore great chunks out of that same London. We found the name (3)_____ in 1940 when special squads of picked men were trained in England to repel invasion and carry out raids. We found (4)_____ _____ in 1940 to identify a group of people within a country who cooperated with the enemy and carried on harassing tactics. And we found (5)_____ in 1943 to name an antitank rocket launcher.

We no longer have wars; we now have "hostile actions," but the new words know better and they keep coming: (6)_____, a nice way to say that hostile action is being intensified or expanded; (7)_____, the ability of a nation to destroy *more than once* every citizen of a hostile nation; (8)_____ _____, a special communication line between the White House and the Kremlin to be used in times of crisis and that will hopefully prevent an "accidental" nuclear war.

Another rich source for words is science. In 1932 came (9)_____, a device that makes electrified particles move at high speeds. A new field today is (10)_____, the science of operating completely by automatic or mechanical means. Our society is rapidly reaching a point at which it could not function without the (11)_____, a machine that performs mathematical operations by mechanical or electrical means and does it with lightning speed; the arrangement of data to be "fed" into this machine is called (12)_____. And within the last few years we developed (13)_____ to describe the process by which we can "see" what is happening in outer space or on the moon even when cameras cannot operate.

All men (and women!) need clothing—and so the fashion and fabric industries constantly create new words. An exceedingly popular synthetic material is called (14)_____, and an older, heavy rayon material is called (15)_____. Wide trousers that look like a skirt are (16)_____, a dress with straight simple lines is a (17)_____, and a skirt that is *very*, *very* short is a (18)_____!

Increased leisure time has made entertainment a major field. Dozens of new words come into our language yearly from this source. A popular one is (19)_____, which comes from the high fidelity sought in radios and phonographs. An intriguing one, (20)_____ _____, is used to describe a close race in which a photograph is necessary to determine the winner. A game of chance, somewhat like lotto, popular with women, is called (21)_____. The use of multiple loudspeakers for greater realism of sound gives us stereophonic sound, or its shortened version, (22)_____. And a form of art that is a favorite with schoolchildren and professional artists is the (23)_____, made by pasting clippings and other materials on a painting or drawing.

Thinking about new words will not only extend your vocabulary; it will also help you to understand the world in which you live, for the words of an age reflect the interests and activities of the people of that age. What do the words of our age tell us about *us*?

18. "I HAVE WORDS TO SPEAK IN THINE EAR . . . ." (*Hamlet*)

Over 400 years ago a man was born who—more than any other individual—had a profound influence on the English language. Single-handedly he created words and phrases, dreamed up sentences that have become proverbs, and showed us the sheer fun of puns and other kinds of wordplay. That man was, of course, William Shakespeare.

Some people think of Shakespeare as a highbrow, an intellectual. He wasn't. He was an average man (who happened to be a genius!), and his plays are loved still because he wrote for the average man. *You* probably quote Shakespeare all the time—but you may not realize it. If you ever talk about "flaming youth" or being "fancy-free," you're quoting Shakespeare. If you ever murmur "too much of a good thing" as three kinds of pie follow the turkey and trimmings, you're quoting Shakespeare. If you ever mutter threateningly, "The worm will turn," you're quoting Shakespeare.

Can you identify the phrases new with Shakespeare but common today that will complete the playlets below? (Hints are given in parentheses.)

I. *Father* (to his son, Bill): Must you have a third helping of roast beef? You're eating me (1)

_____ ____ _____ _____ _____ (*into poverty*)!

Bill: A (2) _____ _____ (*sad vision*) when a father begrudges food for his

own (3) _____ _____ _____ (*close kin*).

Father: Don't live in a (4) _____ _____ (*Eden for a simpleton*), Son.

In this (5) _____ _____ (*ordinary life*) he who would eat

must work!

II. *Chuck:* So I (1) _____ ____ _____ _____ ____ _____ (*show feelings

openly*)! Why should you care? Or do I see the (2) _____

_____ (*symbol of jealousy*) leering over your shoulder?

Frank: Me jealous? Haven't you heard? I'm a (3) _____ _____ _____

(*popular with the girls*)!

Chuck: Oh, you're a (4) _____ _____ _____ (*something that creates a

short-lived sensation*), you are! And who's the lucky girl tonight?

Frank: (boastfully) A (5) _____ _____ _____ _____ _____ (*concoction suitable

for divine beings*)! (Then, after Chuck leaves, Frank adds wistfully, "Well, my sister

is attractive.")

III. *Son* (to father): I need money. I have an (1) _____ _____ (*part of hand irritated

by uneasy sensation*).

Father: In my (2) _____ _____ (*youth*) when a boy needed money, he went to work.

Son: I know you're a (3) _____ _____ _____ (*tall symbol of vigor*),

Dad, but the (4) _____ _____ (*unpleasant aspect*) of life doesn't appeal to me. I'd rather (5) _____ ____ _____ (*expire very slowly*) than get a job.

Father: Then (6) _____ _____ _____ (*exhale a final breath*), my boy. I have a (7) _____ ____ _____ (*generous spirit*) but my wallet is empty!

Son: In you the (8) _____ ____ _____ _____ (*liquid symbolizing generosity*) has run dry! Then work I must!

Father: Don't be upset. I'll (9) _____ _____ (*bet*) you'll like work if you try it.

Son: Well, that's (10) _____ _____ (*a chilling sort of consolation*)!

Bonus: Here are some words that Shakespeare created that *didn't* take.

> smilet—a little smile
> summer's tanlings—suntanned children
> razorable—of a youth ready to be shaved
> birthdom—one's native place
> pensived—saddened

Perhaps it isn't too late to add them now! They might yet become *household words* (*Henry V*)!

19. PROPER NAMES

One way to appreciate the power of connotation is to consider some proper names. Some proper names signify more than the persons who originally bore them. These names may even be used to describe certain kinds of persons.

I. What type of person is suggested by each of the following names?

--- 1. a Napoleon

--- 2. a Hitler

--- 3. a Pontius Pilate

--- 4. a Socrates

--- 5. a Caesar

--- 6. a Joan of Arc

--- 7. a Machiavelli

--- 8. an Annie Oakley

--- 9. a Daniel Boone

--- 10. an Edison

II. Fiction, too, has given us names that are so characteristic, so "right," that they have become part of our language. What do we mean by each of the following?

--- 1. a Galahad

--- 2. a Frankenstein

--- 3. a Shylock

--- 4. a Babbitt

--- 5. a Romeo

--- 6. a Pollyanna

--- 7. a Robin Hood

--- 8. a Simon Legree

--- 9. a Scarlett O'Hara

--- 10. a Mrs. Malaprop

III. What is suggested by these names from the Bible?

--- 1. a Goliath

--- 2. a Job

--- 3. a Cain

-- 4. an Ishmael

-- 5. a Jezebel

-- 6. a Samson

-- 7. a Jonah

-- 8. a Judas

-- 9. a Daniel

-- 10. a Solomon

IV. What do these names from mythology signify?

-- 1. a Hercules

-- 2. a Venus

-- 3. an Adonis

-- 4. a Mars

-- 5. a Titan

V. What is denoted by these names from *geography*?

-- 1. a Waterloo

-- 2. a Gethsemane

-- 3. a Rock of Gibraltar

-- 4. a Marathon

-- 5. a Pearl Harbor

Can you think of any other proper nouns that have a popular significance?

20. ALLUSIONS

A natural follow-up to a discussion of proper names that have become words is a discussion of allusions. An *allusion* is a reference to an historical or literary event or personage. Allusions are used in poems and paintings, in newspaper headlines and political speeches. Why? For several reasons, but the most important one is that a one- or two-word allusion can often take the place of a ten- or twenty-word sentence.

If, for example, you want to say that a woman is beautiful, has the ability to turn men into beasts, and can lure them to destruction, you will use almost twenty words. Instead you can simply say that she is a *Circe*. Circe, a demigoddess of ancient Greece, was beautiful and turned Odysseus' men into swine. Anyone who knows the story of Circe (and many people do) knows immediately the kind of woman you are talking about when you mention a Circe.

I. In this exercise you are given a sentence using an allusion and then a brief explanation of the story behind the allusion. If you look closely at the story, you should be able to discover the meaning of the allusion within the sentence.

1. *a.* Vietnam was President Johnson's *Achilles' heel*.
   b. When Achilles was an infant, his mother dipped him into the river Styx. This made him invulnerable to injury except on the heel, which his mother was holding. Hence, his heel was his one weak point—the one place he could be seriously injured.

   c. Meaning of allusion in 1*a*: _____

   _____

2. *a.* To give the graduating seniors an extended lunch period instead of the beach party they requested is, indeed, to throw a *sop to Cerberus*.
   b. Cerberus was a vicious three-headed dog that guarded the entrance to Hades. To distract him and to placate him, people sometimes threw him a handful of muck—just enough to keep him quiet for a bit.

   c. Meaning of allusion in 2*a*: _____

   _____

   _____

3. *a.* The multimillionaire wondered, with satisfaction, if he truly had the *Midas touch*.
   b. Midas, a king of Phrygia, asked for and received a special gift—everything he touched turned to gold.

   c. Meaning of allusion in 3*a*: _____

   _____

   _____

4. *a.* His *protean* personality fascinated his friends but at the same time caused them to distrust him.
   b. Proteus was a sea-god who could change his shape at will.

   c. Meaning of allusion in 4*a*: _____

   _____

5. *a.* A *pyrrhic* victory is the only kind of victory possible in a nuclear war.
   b. Pyrrhus, an ancient king, won a battle but during the battle suffered very heavy losses.

   c. Meaning of allusion in 5*a*: _____

   _____

6. *a.* The present school curriculum seems to some students a *procrustean* bed.
   b. A legendary Greek highwayman, Procrustes, tied his victims to a bed, then stretched or cut off their legs to make them fit it.

   c. Meaning of allusion in 6*a*: _____

   _____

   _____

7. *a.* *Travels With Charley*, John Steinbeck's report of the people and places encountered on his cross-country trip, might well be subtitled "An American *Odyssey*."
   b. Odysseus, a Greek hero, made a ten-year journey from Troy to his home in Ithaca. During this journey he had many adventures and overcame many dangers, thus gaining knowledge of himself and his world.

   c. Meaning of allusion in 7*a*: _____

   _____

   _____

8. *a.* Some poets, comically, hope to arrive at the height of *Parnassus* by way of a jet plane!
   b. Parnassus was a mountain in ancient Greece sacred to Apollo and the Muses; hence, it symbolizes the font of inspiration and the arts.

   c. Meaning of allusion in 8*a*: _____

   _____

9. *a.* Thanks to her agent, a veritable *Pygmalion*, she was transformed from an ugly duckling into a Hollywood beauty.
   b. Pygmalion was a sculptor who created a statue of a woman so beautiful that, when it was brought to life through the intercession of the gods, he fell in love with it.

   c. Meaning of allusion in 9*a*: _____

   _____

   _____

10. *a.* A teen-ager's attempts to win peer approval *and* parental approval may make him feel he is steering a course between *Scylla and Charybdis*.
    b. Scylla was a rock and Charybdis a whirlpool on opposite sides of a narrow channel. Ships steering between them had to avoid both dangers.

    c. Meaning of allusion in 10*a*: _____

    _____

    _____

II. This time you are given only sentences using allusions. How many can you interpret correctly?

1. *a.* The preparation of the *Oxford English Dictionary* was a *herculean* task.

   b. Meaning of allusion in 1*a*: _____

   _____

   _____

2. *a.* "We have every hope," said the director of the space program, "that with the help of modern science no present-day *Icarus* will fall."

   b. Meaning of allusion in 2*a*: _____

   _____

   _____

3. *a.* The landlord warned the young man applying for the apartment that he would not tolerate any *bacchanalian* parties.

   b. Meaning of allusion in 3*a*: _____

   _____

4. *a.* Standing in Times Square for the first time, he felt like a pygmy surrounded by *cyclopean* structures.

   b. Meaning of allusion in 4*a*: _____

   _____

5. *a.* To decrease air pollution in our cities without infringing on individual freedoms requires a *Solomon*, indeed!

   b. Meaning of allusion in 5*a*: _____

   _____

   _____

6. *a.* The *Argus-eyed* proctor certainly contributed to the honesty of the candidates.

   b. Meaning of allusion in 6*a*: _____

   _____

7. *a.* Tired of political dodges, the would-be candidate decided to *cut the Gordian knot* by announcing that he would run.

   b. Meaning of allusion in 7*a*: _____

   _____

   _____

8. *a.* The United States is a *Goliath* among nations, but more than one small country may be a potential *David*.

   b. Meaning of allusion in 8*a*: _____

   _____

   _____

9. *a.* My personal *nectar* is coconut milk—or perhaps apricot juice. It is hard to decide.

   b. Meaning of allusion in 9*a*: _____

   _____

10. *a.* "*Beware of Greeks bearing gifts*," I warned myself silently, as I accepted an exquisitely wrapped gift from my arch-rival.

    b. Meaning of allusion in 10*a*: _____

    _____

    _____

Part II. *Word Groups*

One of the oldest memory tricks is *association*. Associate a telephone number with an historical year; associate a new name with a facial feature of the owner; associate a place for an appointment with outrageous or silly words. So, to remember CO 1-1492, we recall *Columbus, 1492*; to remember Flora Beakman, we recall her *florid nose*; to remember Westbury, we recall that out *West* they *bury* prairie dogs!

The association we are using in Part II is a little different—and much simpler. We associate words primarily by subject matter. *Biodegradable* may seem difficult, but when you *see* it and *use* it with other *ecological* terms, it fits into a logical niche and becomes memorable. The next time you begin discussing air pollution or detergents with your friends, you will find *associated* words coming easily to mind. And, of course, each time you *use* these words, you are re-enforcing your understanding of them.

In addition, we think you will find the groups themselves interesting. Religion, foods, and crime are traditional subjects that interest most people. Painting, music, and architecture are humanities-related, and therefore of universal interest. And astrology, witches, and boats, while more esoteric, are almost always fascinating to earthbound mortals!

Thinking about these words *in groups*, learning them, and using them in conversation and in writing will yield rich dividends in the form of a more sophisticated, more up-to-date vocabulary.

1. THE AGE OF AQUARIUS

Astrology, a study of the influence of the stars on humans and human affairs, is at least as old as recorded history. In some ages it has been considered a science, a body of true knowledge; hence, a valid guide. In other ages it has been called a pseudoscience, a false knowledge; hence, not trustworthy. If he knows your zodiac sign (better yet, the exact time and date of your birth), an astrologer will cast your horoscope—a profile of your personality traits and a prediction of future events and problems.

On the next page is a chart of the twelve signs of the zodiac. (The zodiac is an imaginary belt in the heavens having twelve divisions.) Each sign of the zodiac covers about one month of the year. The first is Aries, the sign of the ram; the second is Taurus, the sign of the bull, etc. On the chart each of the twelve divisions bears first the name, second the sign, third the birth dates covered by the sign, and fourth six of the personality traits often associated with the sign. Hence, (1) the first division is Aries, the sign is the ram, (2) the dates are Mar. 21 to Apr. 20, and (3) astrologers claim that an Aries is individualistic, has leadership ability and initiative, has strong will power, is proud (even arrogant), and is flirtatious.

Naturally no one can promise you that an introduction to astrology will make you prosperous or wise, but you can be certain that this chapter will help to give you one kind of magic—the magic of word power. It will amuse you, too. As a beginning, become familiar with the entire chart—but you will probably be most interested in *your own* sign of the zodiac!

Now let's see how well you can interpret a zodiac chart.

I. Some words are related to the names of the zodiac divisions. See if you can match the words in the first column with the definitions in the second column. Use the chart (name and sign of each division) as clues.

> *Example:* piscary = a fishing place
> (*Explanation:* The *pisc* also appears in *Pisc*es, and the sign of *Pisc*es is the fish.)

---- 1. aquatic	*a.* to become double
---- 2. leonine	*b.* innocence; purity
---- 3. to geminate	*c.* a spider with a venomous sting
---- 4. piscatorial	*d.* in or on water
---- 5. sagitate	*e.* a glass tank for fish
---- 6. to librate	*f.* characteristic of a lion
---- 7. taurine	*g.* shaped like an arrow
---- 8. scorpion	*h.* to balance
---- 9. aquarium	*i.* bull-like
---- 10. virginity	*j.* pertaining to fishing

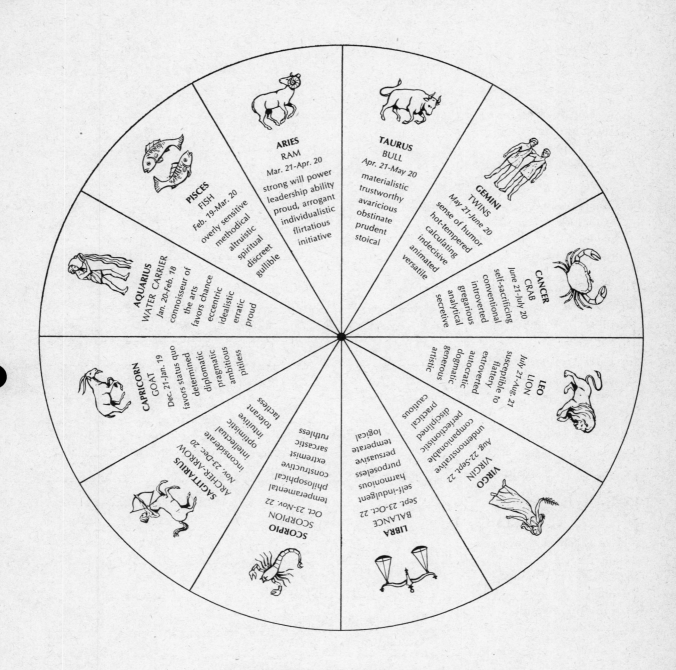

THE SIGNS OF THE ZODIAC

II. Below are the definitions of some personality traits. Use the chart (and a dictionary) to identify each personality trait and the sign of the zodiac with which it is associated.

Example: agreeable; sociable = companionable = Virgo

DEFINITIONS	TRAITS	SIGNS
1. interested in people and things outside oneself		
2. without mercy		
3. able to know by sensing and feeling		
4. unselfish; thoughtful of others		
5. independent of others in thought and action		
6. inclined to direct one's thoughts inward		
7. having several abilities		
8. stubborn		
9. unlikely to show one's feelings		
10. moderate; not excessive		
11. asserting opinion as if it were fact		
12. unusual, strange		
13. tactful; skillful in managing people		
14. overbearing; lordly		
15. lively; full of spirit		
16. hopeful; sanguine		
17. easily fooled or imposed on		
18. passive; not showing one's feelings		
19. mindful of results; practical		
20. greedy		

2. PROFESSIONALS AND PRACTITIONERS

Every human being is interested in other human beings; this is the human condition. Because this is true, you should find enjoyable a journey through the luxuriant jungle of modern specialists. Some of these terms you must know simply to cope with today's world; others will broaden your knowledge further; a few are esoteric but interesting.

I. The specialists with whom you are most likely to come into contact are from the medical profession. You probably know many of them already. Test yourself.

Which doctor would you call if . . .

----------------------------- 1. someone is having a baby?

----------------------------- 2. a child is ill?

----------------------------- 3. a patient needs ether?

----------------------------- 4. someone breaks an ankle?

----------------------------- 5. your feet hurt?

----------------------------- 6. someone needs an operation?

----------------------------- 7. you get a rash?

----------------------------- 8. you fear you have a nervous disorder?

----------------------------- 9. someone has a heart attack?

----------------------------- 10. a friend has a severe earache?

II. Still in the medical realm, see if you can find in the list below the specialists needed to complete sentences 1–14.

dentist	internist	intern
ophthalmologist	psychoanalyst	orthodontist
general practitioner	hematologist	psychiatrist
alienist	freudian	optometrist
psychologist	gynecologist	

1. A family doctor is called a(n) ----------------------------- .

2. A doctor who specializes in women's illnesses is a(n) ----------------------------- .

3. A young doctor, not yet licensed, who works in a hospital under supervision is a(n) ----------------------------- .

4. A doctor who specializes in nonsurgical illnesses is called a(n) ----------------------------- .

5. For regular care of your teeth you would go to a(n) ----------------------------- , but

6. For alignment of irregular teeth you would probably go to a(n) ----------------------------- .

7. If you suspect you have a disease of the eyes, you would visit a(n) ----------------------------- .

8. If you wanted a prescription for glasses, you would visit a(n) _____.

9. Someone who studies mental activity and behavior in human beings is a(n) _____ _____.

10. Someone who studies the treatment of mental disease is a(n) _____.

11. Someone who investigates the unconscious mental processes is a(n) _____ _____.

12. Someone who specializes in the study of the blood is a(n) _____.

13. A psychiatrist who specializes in giving legal evidence is a(n) _____.

14. One who follows the doctrines of Sigmund Freud is called a(n) _____.

III. Can you match the following specialists (nonmedical this time!) with their occupations?

SPECIALISTS	OCCUPATIONS
____ 1. anthropologist	*a.* a student of plant life
____ 2. astronomer	*b.* one who collects and studies coins
____ 3. biologist	*c.* one who studies the origin and development of mankind
____ 4. botanist	*d.* one who concentrates on the meaning and changes of meaning of words
____ 5. geologist	
____ 6. sociologist	*e.* one who studies the origin and history of words
____ 7. archaeologist	*f.* a student of linguistics
____ 8. graphologist	*g.* one who studies the earth, especially rocks
____ 9. zoologist	*h.* a scientific observer of the celestial bodies
____ 10. entomologist	*i.* one who collects and studies stamps
____ 11. etymologist	*j.* one who studies insects
____ 12. philologist	*k.* one who studies the functioning of human society
____ 13. semanticist	*l.* one who studies the science of living matter
____ 14. philatelist	*m.* one who studies animals
____ 15. numismatist	*n.* one who studies past human life and activities as shown by the monuments and relics left by ancient peoples
	o. one who studies handwriting, especially as it reflects character

3. DINNER DATA

You enter a restaurant. The hostess shows you to a table. You open a menu. Then the fun begins! Between French importations and regional specialties, you find your head awhirl. What will you have? More accurately, what do *they* have?

Study the menu on this and the next page. If you are starving, spend some time just enjoying it! Then go on and see how many of the questions on it you can answer.

But before you do, start with hors d'oeuvres. Hors d'oeuvres, as you know, are relishes or tidbits, served before dinner. Here, then, is a "tidbit" matching question that covers a few culinary terms not included on the menu.

____	1. demitasse	*a.*	a connoisseur of delicate viands
____	2. buffet	*b.*	one who eats voraciously
____	3. table d'hôte	*c.*	pertaining to good eating
____	4. soupe du jour	*d.*	the main dish at lunch or dinner
____	5. à la carte	*e.*	food spread on tables from which guests serve themselves
____	6. culinary	*f.*	the soup of the day
____	7. gastronomic	*g.*	a meal of prearranged courses served at a fixed time and price
____	8. gourmet	*h.*	each dish listed separately, with a separate price
____	9. entrée	*i.*	pertaining to cookery
____	10. glutton	*j.*	a small cup of black coffee

MENU

Appetizers

Marinated North Sea Herring	Consommé Julienne
Pâté de Foie Gras Canapés	Borscht
Bouillabaisse	Chicken Gumbo
Manhattan Clam Chowder	Minestrone
French Onion Soup With Croutons	Vichyssoise

Entrées

Salmon Soufflé	Chicken Croquettes
Roast Prime Ribs of Beef au Jus	Pork Chop Suey
Shrimp au Gratin	Mixed Grill
Calf's Liver en Brochette	Duck à la Creole
Turtle Ragoût	Sautéed Salisbury Steak

Vegetables

Baked Stuffed Potato
Sweet Potato Croquettes
Green Corn Succotash
Jerusalem Artichokes
Sliced New Beets

Desserts

Baked Alaska
Chocolate Blanc Mange
Pecan Pralines
Eclair
Maple Parfait

Crêpe Suzette
Petits Fours
Quince and Apricot Compote
Almond Rum Torte
Sherry Trifle

Appetizers

Which appetizer, as listed on the menu, . . .

1. is a Russian soup containing beets, served hot or chilled?

_____

2. is served with small cubes of toasted bread?

_____

3. is a highly seasoned fish stew made with several kinds of fish?

_____

4. was steeped in a seasoned vinegar-oil mixture before cooking?

_____

5. is a clear soup that contains vegetables cut into thin strips?

_____

6. is a soup or stew made of clams and vegetables?

_____

7. consists of crackers or thin pieces of toast spread with a paste made of goose livers?

_____

8. is a chicken soup thickened with okra pods?

_____

9. is a creamy potato and onion soup, usually served cold?

_____

10. is a soup containing vegetables, vermicelli, and herbs in a meat or vegetable broth?

_____

Entreés

Which entrée . . .

1. is a highly seasoned stew of meat and vegetables?

----

2. consists of small pieces of meat cooked with bean sprouts and other vegetables and served with rice?

----

3. is served in its natural juice or gravy?

----

4. is served with a sauce made with stewed tomatoes, peppers, onions, etc.?

----

5. is broiled on a skewer?

----

6. consists of two or more kinds of meat broiled with vegetables or fruit?

----

7. is minced meat dipped in beaten egg and bread crumbs and fried in deep fat?

----

8. is served with cheese?

----

9. has been fried lightly and quickly?

----

10. is a delicate, spongy hot dish, lightened by stiffly beaten whites of eggs?

Desserts

Which dessert . . .

1. is a jellylike preparation of milk thickened with cornstarch or gelatin, and flavored?

----

2. is small frosted tea cakes?

----

3. is cake soaked in wine, with jam or fruit and whipped cream?

----

4. is a thin pancake, usually rolled, with hot orange sauce and flavored with a liqueur?

----

5. is a mixture of whipped cream and egg, frozen and flavored?

----

6. is a dish of fruits cooked in syrup?

----

7. is a light, tubular pastry filled with cream or custard and topped with icing?

----

8. is a sponge cake, filled with vanilla ice cream, covered with meringue, and placed in a hot oven until a delicate brown?

----

9. is a cake in which ground nuts are substituted for flour?

----

10. is a confection of nut kernels roasted in boiling sugar until brown and crisp?

----

4. HOUSEHOLD TERMS

Some of these household terms may be familiar; others may not. But all of them appear regularly —in books about home decorating, in cookbooks, in magazine articles, even in novels. How many do you know? More important, how many could you recognize?

First read these household terms and their definitions:

1. *decanter:* a vessel, often an ornamental bottle, from which wine, water, or another liquid is served at the table.

2. *carafe:* a bottle for water or coffee, also used in serving at the table. In some restaurants small individual carafes are used. These small carafes usually hold two cupfuls of coffee.

3. *cruet:* a glass bottle containing vinegar or salad oil, placed on the table to allow individual seasoning of salads.

4. *tureen:* a large, deep dish with a cover, placed on the dinner table and usually used to serve soup or stew.

5. *ewer:* a pitcher with a wide spout. Today it is generally attractively made and used for pouring liquids. Formerly it was used to hold water for ablutions.

6. *colander:* a strainer, used in cooking, for draining off liquids. A colander is used, for example, in preparing spaghetti.

7. *demijohn:* a large small-necked bottle, usually cased in wickerwork. Today it is often used as a decanter or as a conversation piece.

8. *porringer:* a dish deeper than a saucer; usually used for serving soup, porridge, rice, etc.

9. *epergne:* an ornamental centerpiece for a table, usually a cluster of small dishes.

10. *chafing dish:* a metal or ovenware dish with a lamp or candle beneath it, for cooking food and keeping it hot.

11. *cornucopia:* a horn-shaped or conical dish or receptacle usually filled with different fruits and nuts. It is a favorite centerpiece for the table on holidays.

12. *salver:* simply another name for a tray.

13. *compotier:* a glass, china, or silver dish having a supporting stem; usually used for serving compotes (fruit stewed in a syrup).

Now look at the sketches on the next page. Can you match each sketch with one of the terms you have just learned?

A. ------------------------------   H. ------------------------------

B. ------------------------------   I. ------------------------------

C. ------------------------------   J. ------------------------------

D. ------------------------------   K. ------------------------------

E. ------------------------------   L. ------------------------------

F. ------------------------------   M. ------------------------------

G. ------------------------------

A

B

C

D

E

F

G

H

I

J

K

L

M

101 Ways to Learn Vocabulary

5. CRIME DOES PAY!

Crime doesn't pay, they used to say; but today crime *does* pay, at least on television and in book publishing. You probably consider yourself quite sophisticated in your knowledge of court terminology, but are you as accurate and complete in your understanding as you think you are? Here are some exercises that will ascertain the extent of your legal "know-how." After you have finished the exercises, you may want to challenge Perry Mason. Then again, you may not . . . .

I. First, you are a young law student. Read the paragraph below.

Bill Jones was sueing *Fred Harper* for $100,000. Harper asked for *trial by his peers*. A number of *people who had seen the accident talked about what they had seen*. Some of *what they said* was *seeming proof*, some *based on what they had been told*. Although all had *promised to tell the truth*, Harper believed one of them was guilty of *swearing to what is untrue*. He approached the *judge* for a consultation.

Now check your knowledge of court terminology by trying to match each of the terms below with a phrase from the above paragraph.

--- 1. hearsay

--- 2. bench

--- 3. circumstantial

--- 4. plaintiff

--- 5. taken the oath

--- 6. witnesses

--- 7. perjury

--- 8. defendant

--- 9. their testimony

--- 10. gave evidence

--- 11. a jury trial

II. This time you are an *alleged* murderer. You have been formally *indicted*, and your *attorney* is preparing your case. He has some questions to ask you.

Att.: Do you have an *alibi*?
You: No.
Att.: Is it true there are five *aliases* under which you operate?
You: No, six.
Att.: Did the police take a *paraffin test*?
You: Yes.
Att.: Were the results positive or negative?
You: Positive.
Att.: They took a *moulage* of the footprint found under the window used for entering. Will it match yours?

You: Yes.

Att.: They've outlined the *modus operandi* on this last job. They're comparing it to the M.O. used in several other still unsolved cases. Will they compare positively?

You: Yes.

Att.: Will they be able to prove *premeditation*?

You: Yes.

(The Attorney shrugs his shoulders hopelessly.)

You: (timidly) Do you think I'll be *acquitted*?

If you understood the interrogation, you should be able to match the italicized words in it with the definitions below.

------------------------------ 1. planning a deed before doing it

------------------------------ 2. a process that determines whether a person has discharged a gun recently

------------------------------ 3. a statement that one was elsewhere when a crime was committed

------------------------------ 4. claimed, but without proof

------------------------------ 5. a manner or mode of operation

------------------------------ 6. assumed names

------------------------------ 7. found not guilty

------------------------------ 8. a plaster impression

------------------------------ 9. a lawyer

------------------------------ 10. charged with an offense

III. Now you are a judge. A student editor is interviewing you. Can you answer his questions?

Judge: Good afternoon.

Student: Good afternoon, Your Honor. Can you tell me the difference between a *felony* and a *misdemeanor*?

Judge: A (1)_____ is a minor crime, while a (2)_____ is considerably more serious.

Student: I see. How about the difference between an *arsonist* and a *pyromaniac*?

Judge: A(n) (3)_____ sets fires maliciously; a(n) (4)_____ sets fires because he is emotionally ill and is fascinated by them.

Student: That's certainly clear! Do *verdict* and *sentence* mean the same thing?

Judge: Definitely not. The (5)_____ is the decision of the jury or judge about the defendant's innocence. The (6)_____ is the punishment, or penalty, imposed by the court.

Student: Is there a difference between *exonerate* and *pardon*?

Judge: A great difference. To (7)_____ is to free from blame completely; to (8)_____ is to forgive, or to remit punishment.

Student: Does every prisoner come up for *pardon*?

101 Ways to Learn Vocabulary

Judge: No. The word you're looking for is (9)_ _ _ _ _ _ _ _ _ _—a conditional release of a prisoner who hasn't completed his sentence but who has been recommended because of good behavior.

Student: One last question, Your Honor. What happens to an alien who is convicted of a crime?

Judge: He often is (10)_ _ _ _ _ _ _ _ _ _ _ _ , that is, forced to leave the country.

Here are some other legal terms you may want to look up:

homicide	writ
vandalism	capital punishment
larceny	exile

6. PAINTING WITH BRUSH AND PEN

Whether you use a brush on canvas to daub patches of vermillion, or a pen on paper to concoct purple prose, you are engaged in the same two-part activity: *to depict*—an impression, an idea, a mood, a fear—and *to communicate*—to the many, to the few, or even to a nonexistent ideal.

All the arts are allied, but painting and writing are first cousins that have parallel histories, go through similar cycles, and use many of the same techniques. Many painters write, and many writers paint. Unlike architects and sculptors, they do not use materials requiring a great deal of space. Whatever the reason, they often find themselves in adjoining ateliers (studios). Being neighbors, they meet and talk, argue about methods and purpose, "borrow" a technique from one medium to try in the other. The result is a terminology that often applies equally well to the two arts.

Below are eight terms describing "schools," or types, of writing and painting. Can you match each term with one of the painter-writer groups described?

allegorical	realistic
expressionistic	romantic
idyllic	satiric
impressionistic	surrealistic

1. Hogarth painted bitter pictures of the social evils of 18th-century England; Swift wrote a bitter novel about many of the same evils. Their works may be described as _____ .

2. Bryant wrote charming poems about Nature; his friend Cole painted charming pictures of Nature. Their works suggest a mood of peace and contentment, and may be described as _____ _____ .

3. Dali, in his paintings, often attempts to depict the working of the subconscious; James Joyce tried to do the same thing in his novel *Finnegans Wake*. Their works may be described as _____ .

4. Sir Walter Scott's novels are imaginative, adventurous, often exotic; Géricault's paintings are vigorous and emotion-laden. Their works may be described as _____ .

5. Van Gogh's swirling sky of *Starry Night* and O'Neill's bars and flaming furnace in *The Hairy Ape* both try to convey the artist's emotional reaction rather than the actual appearance of the object depicted. The result is often deliberate distortion and may be described as _____ _____ .

6. Verlaine in his poetry and Monet in his paintings tried to depict a scene as it *appeared to the artist* at a particular moment. Their work may be described as _____ .

7. Courbet painted detailed, factual scenes of village life in Ornans; Sinclair Lewis wrote detailed, true-to-life novels about businessmen and lawyers in the United States. Both tried to avoid idealization. Their works may be described as _____ .

8. Breughel in his painting *The Parable of the Blind*, and Dante in his epic poem *The Divine Comedy*, are depicting scenes intended to point out the danger of sin to man. Both works present a concrete

narrative capable of being interpreted in an abstract or spiritual way. Therefore, the works may be described as _____.

These are some terms common to both writing and painting. Can you match term with definition?

style   classic
caricature   composition
motif

9. The organization of the different parts of a work of art (any kind) to achieve a unified whole is called _____.

10. A dominant or recurrent idea, feature, or theme in a work of art is called a _____ _____.

11. A ludicrous exaggeration of a peculiarity or defect of a person or place is called a _____ _____.

12. The particular, distinctive, or characteristic form used in the creation of a work of art is called _____.

13. A work of art generally accepted over a period of time to be of the first rank is called a _____.

Some adjectives can be used effectively to describe a painting or a literary work. Try to match the adjectives with the works described.

didactic   melodramatic
eclectic   memorable
erudite   panoramic
esoteric   provocative
maudlin   urbane

14. A work of art that is overly sentimental and weepy is _____.

15. A work of art that attempts to teach rather than simply to express is _____.

16. A work of art that stimulates thought and sometimes action is _____.

17. A work of art that is easily remembered is _____.

18. A work of art that is profound and meant only for the select few is _____.

19. A work of art that is the result of selecting and using techniques of several "schools" is _____.

20. A work of art that overuses passion, coincidence, and sentiment is _____.

21. A work of art that is learned, or scholarly, is _____.

22. A work of art that comprehensively surveys a landscape or subject is _____.

23. An elegant, refined, or polished work of art is _____.

Here are some miscellaneous but pertinent terms:

anonymous   pseudonym
forgery   triptych
plagiarism   trilogy
primitive

24. A three-part painting is called a _____.

25. A three-part work of literature is called a _____.

26. In literature, if one copies another's writing without giving credit to the original writer, one is guilty of _____.

27. In painting, if one copies another's painting and signs it with the original artist's name, one is guilty of _____.

28. If any work of art or literature is not signed, it is said to be by a(n) _____ artist.

29. If any artist or writer uses, to sign his work, a name other than his own, the assumed name is called a(n) _____.

30. The style of an artist or writer working in the simple, crude style of an earlier age is called _____.

7. MUSICAL MOMENTS

"If music be the food of love, play on," said Shakespeare. And since everyone loves a lover, everyone—to some extent—must love music. Music and its rhythms are the base of life; music and its melodies are the ornaments of life. We walk with an unheard beat, talk with a cadence, meet joy with a song, calm grief with a dirge. Since music is with us at all times, we should be familiar with its terminology so that we can be as "at home" with music as music is "at home" with us.

I. Musical Voices

There are all kinds of voices—male voices and female voices, high voices and low voices, single voices and multiple voices. Can you match the voices in the first column with the definitions in the second column?

____	1. alto (contralto)	*a.*	a person who has unusual technical skill
____	2. tenor	*b.*	middle female voice
____	3. bass	*c.*	four voices or instruments
____	4. baritone	*d.*	lowest male voice
____	5. falsetto	*e.*	lowest female voice
____	6. soprano	*f.*	one voice or instrument
____	7. mezzo-soprano	*g.*	a soprano who can sing ornate melodies
____	8. solo	*h.*	highest female voice
____	9. quartet	*i.*	unnaturally high pitched male voice
____	10. duet	*j.*	middle male voice
____	11. coloratura	*k.*	two voices or instruments
____	12. virtuoso	*l.*	highest natural adult male voice

II. Musical Instruments

There are all kinds of musical instruments, too: *strings*, like the violin, the viola, the cello, and the bass viol; *woodwinds*, like the bassoon, the clarinet, the piccolo, the oboe, and the flute; *drums*, like the timpani; and *brasses*, like the trumpet, the trombone, and the French horn. Below is an alphabetical list of the instruments just named. Look at the sketches on the next page, and see if you can match the instruments with the names. Simply insert the letter of the instrument on the blank before the appropriate name.

____ 1. bass viol		____ 6. flute		____ 11. trumpet
____ 2. bassoon		____ 7. French horn		____ 12. viola
____ 3. cello		____ 8. oboe		____ 13. violin
____ 4. clarinet		____ 9. piccolo		
____ 5. drum		____ 10. trombone		

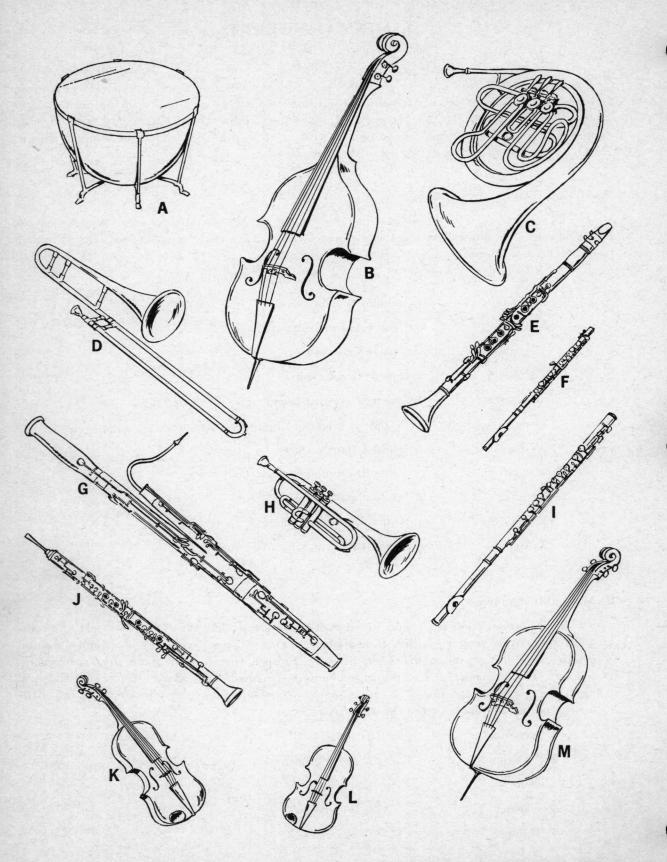

101 Ways to Learn Vocabulary

III. Musical Forms

Finally, there are musical forms. Below are fifteen such forms, all regularly used. Can you associate each form with the appropriate definition?

aria	étude	overture
cantata	madrigal	serenade
carol	opera	sonata
choral	operetta	suite
concerto	oratorio	symphony

---------------- 1. a drama mostly sung, accompanied by orchestra

---------------- 2. a light musical-dramatic work

---------------- 3. an elaborate instrumental composition for a full orchestra

---------------- 4. a composition, usually in symphonic form, in which one or several instruments stand out against the orchestra

---------------- 5. an orchestral composition, usually an introduction to an opera, oratorio, etc.

---------------- 6. a dramatic text, often on a theme from Scripture, set to music with orchestral accompaniment

---------------- 7. an elaborate melody sung by a single voice

---------------- 8. a poem or narrative set to music to be sung by a chorus and soloists

---------------- 9. a song of joy; a joyful hymn

---------------- 10. an instrumental composition built upon a single musical technique

---------------- 11. an unaccompanied rendition of a lyrical poem, usually in several parts

---------------- 12. an instrumental musical composition typically of three or four movements in contrasting rhythms and keys

---------------- 13. music sung outdoors at night, often beneath a lady's window

---------------- 14. a modern instrumental composition in several movements

---------------- 15. a hymn tune or a harmonization of a traditional melody

8. SHOW BIZ

You are a director. You are in the process of planning and producing the most spectacular film of the year. Naturally you have a few problems.

I. Your first major problem is to decide what kind of movie you are going to direct:

spine chiller   soap opera

cliff-hanger   animated film

spectacular

Before you make a decision, you must be familiar with each type. Match the terms in the above list with the definitions below.

-   1. a sentimental tearjerker

-   2. a Hitchcock type mystery

-   3. a lavish show with lots of extras and props

-   4. a hand-drawn film using no real actors

-   5. an adventure that keeps the spectator in suspense through many exciting episodes

II. Your second problem is casting:

stand-in   stunt man

ingenue   extra

script girl

From the above list whom would you "cast" for

-   1. the part of a naive young girl?

-   2. a substitute for the leading man during an auto accident scene?

-   3. each of the hundred soldiers used in one scene as background?

-   4. a substitute to take the place of the leading lady while lighting is being tried, cameras focused, etc.?

-   5. someone to keep track of details, such as the dress the star wears during a certain scene, the date of the newspaper used as a prop, etc.?

III. Now you are confronted with some new problems:

ad lib   cue

upstage   set

props

1. The opening scene takes place in front of an old Western saloon. You don't need a whole saloon, but you do need an appropriate - - - - - - - - - - - - - - -.

2. In that first scene you need a couple of guns, a horse blanket, a saddle, and a large sign. In other words, you need certain _ _ _ _ _ _ _ _ _ _ _ _ _ _ .

3. The hero wants to know if, during the fight, he can depart from the script and add dialogue of his own, or _ _ _ _ _ _ _ _ _ _ _ _ _ _ .

4. The villain, inexperienced, forgets his entrances and exits and needs someone to _ _ _ _ _ _ _ _ _ _ _ him.

5. Without realizing it, you hired one extra who keeps trying to _ _ _ _ _ _ _ _ _ _ _ _ _ the hero by moving to the back of the set, thus forcing the hero to face away from the audience.

IV. You have a conference with the cameramen. They want to know what kind of camera work you want in certain scenes:

close-up   long shot
fade-out   dissolve
panning

_ _ _ _ _ _ _ _ _ _ _ _ _ _ _ _ _ _ 1. a scene showing a large crowd in the distance

_ _ _ _ _ _ _ _ _ _ _ _ _ _ _ _ _ _ 2. a scene in which miles of country are shown slowly, from west to east

_ _ _ _ _ _ _ _ _ _ _ _ _ _ _ _ _ _ 3. a scene showing the grief-stricken face of the leading lady

_ _ _ _ _ _ _ _ _ _ _ _ _ _ _ _ _ _ 4. a scene in which a Western street grows darker until the screen is entirely black

_ _ _ _ _ _ _ _ _ _ _ _ _ _ _ _ _ _ 5. a scene in which the hero's face begins to disappear, but before it disappears completely, the villain's face appears

V. The film is finally finished. But you still have a few problems to solve:

rave   SRO
angel   dub in
straw-hat circuit

1. The film is showing in one theater. There are more people than there are seats. What sign do you have put up in the lobby? _ .

2. The critics love it. They praise the acting, the directing, the story, the sound track. Your publicity man wants to know how he should describe the reviews. You say, "Call them _ reviews!"

3. Foreign theaters want it. You decide to _ new dialogue in French and Italian.

4. Then you decide to take it to Broadway, that is, to prepare it for stage production. You are momentarily without funds, so you seek a(n) _ .

5. It is also successful as a play. After a run of twenty-two months on Broadway, you send it out on the _ , where it plays in barns and summer theaters.

9. WITCHES' BREW

Once upon a time witches could be seen gathering on Walpurgis Night (the eve of May Day) in the Harz Mountains in Germany for the witches' Sabbath. Once upon a time wizards were consulted by leaders of government, and astrologers influenced world events. If these things seem bizarre (outlandish, peculiar) today, they shouldn't. For the second half of the twentieth century has seen a rekindling of interest in the occult arts.

On more than one college campus warlocks conjure, and in the cities witches brew magic potions and cast spells. In such circumstances it is wise to know some of the terminology associated with witchcraft.

First, there are the major branches of the occult art:

1. demonology—belief in demons, or devils
2. alchemy—the art of transforming base metals into gold
3. necromancy—the art of reading the future by communicating with the dead
4. lycanthropy—the kind of witchcraft in which a person takes on the form and nature of an animal, especially a wolf

Next, there are the people associated with magic. Can you match each type of person with his "occupation"?

____ 1. witch	*a.* a male witch; a wizard; a sorcerer
____ 2. warlock	*b.* one who believes a person can speak to the dead through a medium
____ 3. spiritualist	
____ 4. magus	*c.* a medicine man in some Indian tribes; one who can summon good and evil spirits
____ 5. mesmerist	*d.* a woman who practices magic
____ 6. astrologer	*e.* one who can "see" things that cannot normally be seen
____ 7. shaman	*f.* a magician, especially a wise one
____ 8. clairvoyant	*g.* one who hypnotizes others
	h. one who predicts the future by the stars

All these practitioners of the black art *do* things. Match their operations with the definitions.

____ 9. to conjure	*a.* to cause to rise into the air and float, in apparent defiance of gravity
____ 10. to levitate	
____ 11. to cast a spell	*b.* to bring spirits from the dead
____ 12. to call up spirits	*c.* to call up a devil by incantation
	d. to bewitch; to take control of another person

To *do* the above things, these magicians must have "spells." Can you match the spells on the next page with their definitions?

_ _ _ _ 13. incantation   *a.* a mystical word used to ward off calamity

_ _ _ _ 14. evil eye   *b.* an object supposed to have magical powers

_ _ _ _ 15. abracadabra   *c.* a chanted verbal formula

_ _ _ _ 16. fetish   *d.* nonsense words used as a formula by some magicians

_ _ _ _ 17. hocus-pocus   *e.* a look capable of inflicting injury

Most spells and magical operations use a physical object to transmit the power involved. Can you match these?

_ _ _ _ 18. philter   *a.* a small doll, often dressed to resemble the person a witch desires to harm

_ _ _ _ 19. amulet

_ _ _ _ 20. poppet   *b.* a potion designed to excite love

_ _ _ _ 21. elixir   *c.* a mixture that prolongs life indefinitely

_ _ _ _ 22. potion   *d.* an ornament or gem worn to ward off bad luck; a talisman

    e. a liquid medicine or poison

Finally, there are certain adjectives used to describe magicians and their art. Can you match these?

_ _ _ _ 23. recondite   *a.* relating to secret knowledge gained from mysterious agencies

_ _ _ _ 24. occult   *b.* relating to knowledge known only to an inner circle or to the initiated

_ _ _ _ 25. esoteric

    c. relating to knowledge too deep for ordinary comprehension

Mix all the above together, simmer in a cauldron (large kettle or pot), and you have a Witches' Brew! Halloween, anyone?

10. ARCHITECTURAL TERMS

A few architectural terms are used so often in newspapers and magazines that you should know what they mean. A knowledge of these terms will help you to be more observant architecturally and will sharpen your descriptions of houses, public buildings, monuments, and other structures. They are well worth knowing. Besides, they will make travel more interesting as you note an especially engaging pilaster or pediment!

First read these common architectural terms and their definitions:

1. *gargoyle:* a spout that projects from the gutter of a building to carry off rainwater. The spout usually terminates in a grotesque animal or human head with a large open mouth.

2. *flying buttress:* a buttress is a prop built against a wall for the purpose of giving it stability. A flying buttress (originally in Gothic architecture) is an arch that carries the thrust of the nave wall to a solid pier buttress.

3. *arch:* usually a curved structure resting on supports at both extremities, used to sustain weight.

4. *keystone:* the wedge-shaped, topmost stone in an arch, regarded as holding the pieces in place; that on which associated things depend.

5. *post-and-lintel:* two upright pieces of timber, metal, or stone (posts) topped by a horizontal piece (lintel); the basic structure of any door or gate.

6. *steeple:* a lofty tower attached to a church or other building, often housing bells.

7. *spire:* the tall, tapering structure that surmounts a steeple (steeple and spire are sometimes used interchangeably).

8. *pylon:* an architectural form of a projecting nature that flanks an entrance; a tower.

9. *pediment:* a low, triangular gable (used especially in the Greek, Roman, and Renaissance periods); often used over a portico or at the ends of a gable-roofed building.

10. *eaves:* the overhanging lower edge of a roof.

11. *pilaster:* a square or rectangular pillar, with capital and base, engaged in a wall from which it projects.

12. *cornice:* a horizontal molded projection that crowns or finishes a wall, building, etc.

Now look at the sketches on the next page. Can you connect each sketch or part of a sketch with one of the definitions you have just read? (If the labeling letter is below the sketch, it refers to the whole sketch. If it is next to a line pointing to one part of a sketch, it refers only to that one part.)

A. _____   G. _____

B. _____   H. _____

C. _____   I. _____

D. _____   J. _____

E. _____   K. _____

F. _____   L. _____

11. RELATED TO RELIGION

A topic of perennial interest to most people is religion. Even if you are not interested in a depth-study of one religion, you probably are interested in the concept of religion and in some aspects of religion.

I. The obvious starting place is the word *theology*: the science of religious knowledge and belief. Theology begins with *theo*, a root meaning *God*. Another word beginning with the same root is *theocracy*, a form of government such as that established by the Puritans. Can you guess what type of men are government leaders in a theocracy? (1)_____

Now let's look at some theological "isms." Can you match each "ism" with its definition?

____ 2. monotheism   *a.* the belief that the entire universe is God

____ 3. polytheism   *b.* belief in one God

____ 4. pantheism   *c.* belief in a personal God who does not influence man

____ 5. deism   *d.* belief in many gods

Next are the buildings in which people worship. Try to match each building with its description.

____ 6. church   *e.* a building used by Jewish communities for public worship

____ 7. mosque   *f.* a cave or niche, often containing a religious statue

____ 8. synagogue   *g.* an Islamic place of public worship

____ 9. cathedral   *h.* a building for public worship, especially for Christians

____ 10. grotto   *i.* the principal church of an area, presided over by a bishop

A church has many parts. Here are some of them. Can you match each term with its definition?

altar	pew
apse	pulpit
belfry	sacristy
choir	spire
nave	steeple

_____ 11. an elevated stand usually reserved for the preacher

_____ 12. the part of the church reserved for singers

_____ 13. a table or similar structure used as a center of worship or ritual

_____ 14. a bell tower

_____ 15. a projecting part of a church, usually semicircular

_____ 16. the long central section of a church

_____ 17. a bench with a back, used by members of the congregation

_____ 18. a tall structure usually having a small spire at the top and surmounting a church tower

_____ 19. a room housing sacred vessels and vestments

_____ 20. a steeply tapering roof sometimes constructed on top of a steeple

76

II. Here are some groups of words often confused. Can you eliminate the confusion by correctly filling each blank?

1. *agnostic* and *atheist*

A(n) _____ denies the existence of God while a(n) _____ considers the existence of God a problem that cannot be solved.

2. *heretic* and *infidel*

A(n) _____ is a non-believer (especially in Christianity) while a(n) _____ is one who dissents from an accepted Christian belief.

3. *diocese, parish*, and *see*

A _____ is the portion of a diocese committed to a particular priest or minister;

a _____ is a district under the authority of a bishop; and a _____ is a diocesan center.

4. *clergy* and *laity*

The _____ are laymen, while the _____ are ordained religious leaders.

5. *apostle* and *disciple*

A(n) _____ is one who receives religious instruction while a(n) _____ is a teacher and a preacher—specifically the Twelve _____ of Christ. Hence, the Twelve were first _____, then _____.

III. What about the leaders in different religions? Their titles vary, as do their duties. Try to match each term in the first column with its definition in the second column.

____ 1. priest   *a.* someone who assists a priest or minister

____ 2. rabbi   *b.* a minor parish officer, especially in Britain, who keeps order in church

____ 3. minister   *c.* the priest or minister *in charge* of a church or parish

____ 4. deacon   *d.* in the Catholic Church an ecclesiastical prince who assists the pope

____ 5. elder   *e.* someone ordained to perform sacred functions (used of Catholic and Episcopal clergy)

____ 6. pastor

____ 7. bishop   *f.* in the Catholic Church the bishop of Rome and the head of the Church

____ 8. cardinal   *g.* a Jewish teacher or doctor of the law

____ 9. pope   *h.* a woman who has taken religious vows

____ 10. monk   *i.* a member of a religious order often dedicated to contemplation

____ 11. beadle   *j.* someone authorized to conduct religious services (used of most Protestant clergy)

____ 12. sexton

____ 13. nun   *k.* an underofficer in a church who rings bells and takes care of church property

l. in some churches, older men who are given special functions

m. a clergyman at the head of a diocese or district

IV. In our civilization one cannot talk about religion for long without mentioning the Bible. Listed below are some biblical terms. Complete the paragraphs about the Bible by writing the correct term in each of the blanks.

Book of Revelation   Famine   parables
Conquest   Genesis   Old Testament
Death   gospels   prophets
Exodus   New Testament   War

The Bible is composed of two main parts: the (1)_____, made up of books about the covenant of God with the Hebrews, and the (2)_____, made up of books about Christ's life and death and the work done by his Apostles after his death.

The Old Testament begins with a book called (3)_____, meaning "beginning" or "origin." The second book is called (4)_____, meaning "departure," the departure of the Jews from Egypt. Important in the Old Testament are (5)_____, men who, inspired by God, publicly declare messages from Him.

The New Testament contains the (6)_____, four books that record Christ's life and doctrines and (7)_____, short allegorical stories that teach spiritual truths. The last book of the New Testament is the Apocalypse, also known as the (8)_____. One of the visions in this book describes the Four Horsemen of the Apocalypse: (9)_____ on a white horse, (10)_____ on a red horse, (11)_____ on a black horse, and (12)_____ on a pale horse. The Four Horsemen have played a part in many literary and artistic works.

V. There are a few other religious terms with which you should be familiar. Can you match the terms in the first column with the definitions in the second column?

____ 1. anathema   *a.* one who sacrifices his life rather than renounce his faith

____ 2. iconoclast   *b.* a sacred song or poem

____ 3. liturgy   *c.* any question-and-answer book

____ 4. psalm   *d.* a curse solemnly pronounced by Church authority

____ 5. homily   *e.* buying or selling ecclesiastical favors

____ 6. ecumenical   *f.* the public rites and services of the Christian church

____ 7. catechism   *g.* stealing or desecrating that which is sacred

____ 8. sacrilege   *h.* a discourse for the purpose of religious instruction

____ 9. martyr   *i.* one who breaks icons (religious images); today, one who attacks any cherished belief

____ 10. simony

j. universal and worldwide, especially as it refers to the unity of religions

You still may not be interested in arguing about how many angels can dance on the head of a pin, but you should be considerably better armed to think about religion and to discuss it with your friends.

12. PSYCHOLOGICAL TERMS

Today few topics evoke such immediate interest as psychology. Most of us use some psychological terms, although we often use them improperly. We cannot resist using them because the human mind both attracts and repels—but it never ceases to enthrall. You will want to know the correct meanings of psychological terms in common use, but a word of warning is in order. After you have learned these words, do *not* use them for intensive analysis of self or others. That is a job for the expert, not for the dilettante!

If you wish to apply this new knowledge, practice on the fictitious characters in novels, movies, and TV programs. This will have a salutary side effect: you will find yourself reading more carefully, thinking more about what you have read, and criticizing, let's hope, with sophistication and perception!

The following terms are those most commonly used. Below the terms are short "case histories." Play the diagnostician: using the given terms, try to complete each description.

Electra complex	neurosis	sadist
euphoria	obsession	schizophrenia
extrovert	Oedipus complex	sibling
introvert	paranoia	therapy
manic-depressive	psychosis	trauma
masochist	psychosomatic	

1. Jane is preoccupied with her own thoughts, behavior, and attitudes; she is a(n) _____.

2. Bob is interested in things, people, and events outside himself; he is a(n) _____ _____.

3. Agatha's tics and many fears indicate a rather mild nervous disorder, a(n) _____ _____.

4. Martin's wild moods and irrational behavior indicate a mental disorder so severe that it is interfering with his functioning normally, either intellectually or socially. He suffers from a(n) _____ _____.

5. Clara's physical illness is _____: that is, it is probably caused by an emotional disorder.

6. William has a constant feeling that he is dirty. He washes his hands repeatedly. In all other aspects of life he behaves rationally, but on this one fixed idea he is irrational. He cannot stop washing his hands and worrying about being dirty. He has a(n) _____.

7. When Jackie was five years old, he saw one man shoot another; because this experience disturbed his emotional development, it is properly called a(n) _____.

8. Melanie feels marvelous; she believes herself (incorrectly) to be the possessor of extraordinary wealth and power. Melanie is in a state of _____.

9. Richard, a young poverty-stricken architect, sometimes thinks he is the emperor of the world; at other times he lives in terror because he believes bands of assassins are pursuing him; he is suffering from a limited psychosis known as _____.

10. Jeremy sometimes is excited and aggressive, even occasionally violent; an hour later he may be sad and lethargic. Forever alternating between these two extreme emotional states, Jeremy may be diagnosed as a(n) _____ .

11. Martha, who enjoys experiencing physical pain or humiliation, is probably a(n) _____ _____ .

12. The opposite of Martha, Timothy enjoys *causing* physical pain or humiliation to others; he is probably a(n) _____ .

13. Dr. M. says that Isabel needs treatment designed to cure or alleviate her emotional disorder; in other words, she needs _____ .

14. Ten-year-old Sue's major problem is _____ rivalry; she fears that her brother Jim and sister Nora are better loved and more talented than she is.

15. Michael hates his father and possesses an excessive and dependent love for his mother; he has a(n) _____ .

16. Tina hates her mother and possesses an excessive and dependent love for her father; she has a(n) _____ .

17. Janet's withdrawal from reality has resulted in erratic and variable behavior. Sometimes (without cause) she is bold, aggressive, almost exuberant; at other times (also without cause) she seems to retreat within herself, refusing to speak to anyone or even to notice the presence of anyone. She unquestionably has a split personality; more technically, she is suffering from _____ _____ .

13. NAUTICAL KNOWLEDGE

Wind blowing your hair, spray stinging your cheeks, taste of salt and smell of brine. . . . Sound good? It does to an increasing number of Americans each year who are flocking to the waterways of the United States as they once flocked to prairie land and mountains.

So many people now operate boats—motorboats, sailboats, rowboats, and cabin cruisers—that out on the bay on a summer Sunday you can get ensnarled in the kind of traffic jam that you are trying to escape.

If you are a boatowner, you already have a nautical vocabulary. But if you are a landlubber, you should acquire at least the basics. If you don't, you may offend a host-boatman unwittingly. There are few crimes more heinous than referring to the "front" or the "back" of a boat; than calling a chart a "map" or a galley a "kitchen"!

Begin acquiring nautical knowledge by trying to identify the parts of the cabin cruiser shown below. Here are the terms you will need:

keel	bow
stern	propeller
cabin	port
hull	starboard
rudder	waterline

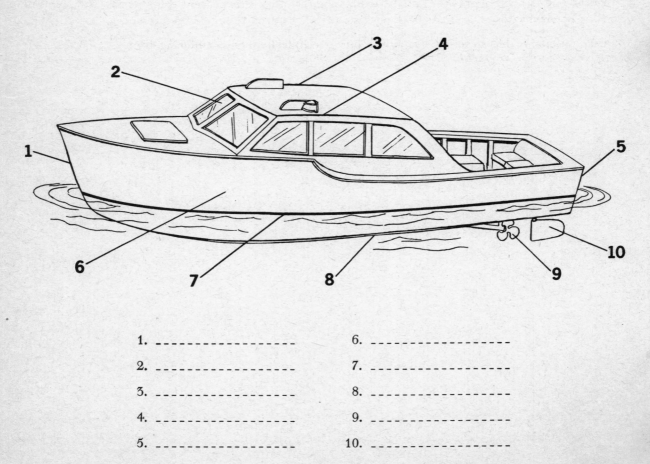

1. _ _ _ _ _ _ _ _ _ _ _ _ _ _ _ _   6. _ _ _ _ _ _ _ _ _ _ _ _ _ _ _

2. _ _ _ _ _ _ _ _ _ _ _ _ _ _ _ _   7. _ _ _ _ _ _ _ _ _ _ _ _ _ _ _

3. _ _ _ _ _ _ _ _ _ _ _ _ _ _ _ _   8. _ _ _ _ _ _ _ _ _ _ _ _ _ _ _

4. _ _ _ _ _ _ _ _ _ _ _ _ _ _ _ _   9. _ _ _ _ _ _ _ _ _ _ _ _ _ _ _

5. _ _ _ _ _ _ _ _ _ _ _ _ _ _ _ _   10. _ _ _ _ _ _ _ _ _ _ _ _ _ _ _

As your next step, master the directions most commonly used.

headway	underway
dead ahead	windward
leeward	forward
aft	abaft
starboard	port

11. On board a boat, the right side, when you face the bow, is called _____.

12. The left side, when you face the bow, is called _____.

13. A boatman, facing the bow, is facing _____.

14. A boatman, facing the stern, is facing _____.

15. A point on the boat that is closer to the stern than another point is _____.

16. _____ is any point toward which the boat is heading on a straight course.

17. If the boat runs *toward* the direction from which the wind blows, it is running _____.

18. If the boat runs *away* from the direction from which the wind blows, it is running _____.

19. When the boat is actually moving through the water, it is said to be _____.

20. When it is moving forward, it is said to be making _____.

There is still a grab bag full of terms with which you should be familiar. Try these:

log	landfall	shipshape
heaves to	fathom	knot
scud	capsizes	founder
list	even keel	yaw
adrift	wake	aground

21. The track left in the water as a result of the boat's movement is called the _____.

22. A boat that is not anchored, not made fast is _____.

23. A boat that touches bottom is _____.

24. A boat that leans to port or starboard is said to _____.

25. A boat that floats as she should, smoothly and evenly, is said to have an _____.

26. A boat that runs off her course (as when struck by a heavy sea) is said to _____.

27. A boat that runs before a gale is said to _____.

28. A boat that turns over _____.

29. A boat that is overwhelmed by heavy seas, and sinks after filling up, is said to _____.

30. One _____ a boat by anchoring it bow to the wind to ride out heavy seas.

31. A _____ is a unit of length, equal to six feet, used in measuring depth of water.

32. A _____ is a unit of speed equivalent to one nautical mile, or a little over 6,000 feet, an hour; it is sometimes loosely used to mean a nautical mile.

33. A book in which all events occurring during a cruise are recorded is called a _____.

34. Coming in from the sea, one's first sight of land is called _____.

35. When everything on board ship is in good order, everything is _____.

    Notice that a nautical vocabulary can be used in nonnautical writing. It can add interest and color if you use it sparingly and well. Can you supply nautical terms for the following nonnautical sentences?

36. A well-balanced person is sometimes said to be on an _____.

37. A woman carrying a camera, binoculars, and a shoulder bag on her right shoulder probably _____ as she walks.

38. A business which was going well but which, encountering problems, collapsed completely might be said to have _____.

39. Someone who is going through life aimlessly, without destination or direction, is _____.

40. If you have been working on a difficult problem but at last you are making progress, you may claim, with elation, that you are making _____.

    Good sailing!

14. WORD CLASSIFICATION LISTS

Word classification lists can be fun, and they can be functional. They will stretch your vocabulary, stimulate your curiosity, and send you searching through the dictionary. Begin simply, with Step I. After you have become an expert, proceed to the full alphabet list. You will find it a challenging pastime for odd moments.

Step I. Fill in as many of the blanks below as possible, following the letters on the left and the column headings. Note that the word already entered in the first blank is *sapphire*—which names a color and begins with *s*.

	COLORS	ANIMALS	LIVING QUARTERS	ARTICLES OF CLOTHING	FLOWERS
S	sapphire				
T					
A					
M					
P					

Step II. Now try this one.

	MAKES OF CARS	POETS	MOVIE STARS	VERBS THAT DESCRIBE TYPES OF FOOT MOVEMENT	MEN'S NAMES
P					
A					
S					
T					
E					

Step III. You are now ready for the "big time"! Try the full alphabet chart on the next page. Remember that you may not be able to fill in *every* rectangle; the fun lies in trying! Remember also that you can vary the categories at the top of the columns. Possibilities are limited only by your imagination!

	COLORS	ANIMALS	FLOWERS	BIRDS	GROUPS	ARTICLES OF CLOTHING	HOUSEHOLD FURNISHINGS	LIVING QUARTERS	CONTAINERS FOR LIQUIDS	VEHICLES
A										
B										
C										
D										
E										
F										
G										
H										
I										
J										
K										
L										
M										
N										
O										
P										
Q										
R										
S										
T										
U										
V										
W										
X										
Y										
Z										

15. WHAT'S IN A NAME? (Part 1)

What's in a name? That which we call a rose
By any other name would smell as sweet.

—Shakespeare (*Romeo and Juliet*)

Names have an inherent fascination for most of mankind. We hold our names precious because they are, somehow, part of us and at the same time a summation of us. In some societies a person's given name is so sacred that it is never spoken, and he is given a second name for daily use. After John F. Kennedy's death, the finest tribute his countrymen could conceive was to name schools, squares, streets, an airport, and even a cape (Cape Kennedy) in his honor. Whole nations have gone to war to uphold the honor of a country's name, and there must be few in this country who have not thrilled at the sound of "America"!

Why are we fascinated by names? Isn't it because a name is an especially rich symbol, a symbol clothed in a million experiences, a symbol embellished by a million associations? A name *is* the object named. Contrary to William Shakespeare, a rose by any other name might smell as sweet, but would not smell quite like a *rose!*

I. Think about first names. Which names are popular in your age group? Recall the first names of your parents, uncles, and aunts. Compare the two lists. Are there any names that are perennial favorites? If so, what is the probable reason? Why do other names go in and out of fashion? Is choice of names influenced by movie stars, politicians, astronauts, royalty? If so, what does this suggest? Can first names affect their owners? Is there a stereotyped idea of what an Abigail is like, or an Elmer? Is the choice of first names influenced by nationality? By section of country? By race? By creed?

II. Everyone has a first name, and many first names have a special meaning. Using dictionaries or word books or your own memory bank, see if you can match the following first names with their meanings.

A. ____ 1. Patrick   *a.* a helmet of resolution

____ 2. Roger   *b.* a rock

____ 3. Richard   *c.* a guardian of property

____ 4. John   *d.* famous with the spear

____ 5. Edward   *e.* beloved

____ 6. Robert   *f.* noble, patrician-like

____ 7. William   *g.* a twin

____ 8. Thomas   *h.* bright in fame

____ 9. David   *i.* God is gracious

____ 10. Peter   *j.* strong like a ruler; powerful

B. ____ 1. Elizabeth   *a.* a weaver

   ____ 2. Deborah   *b.* grace

   ____ 3. Dorothy   *c.* rejuvenation

   ____ 4. Gertrude   *d.* consecrated to God

   ____ 5. Irene   *e.* a queen

   ____ 6. Margaret   *f.* a spear maiden

   ____ 7. Penelope   *g.* a bee

   ____ 8. Regina   *h.* a pearl

   ____ 9. Edna   *i.* a gift of God

   ____ 10. Ann   *j.* peace

III. Many first names (full name or shortened form) have a separate dictionary meaning when not capitalized. Can you find first names that will also fit the following definitions?

> *Example:* a piece of money of little value
> *Answer:* Penny

_____ 1. to initiate legal proceedings

_____ 2. good judgment; discretion

_____ 3. a visible impression upon anything, like a line

_____ 4. the winner in a contest

_____ 5. a smooth, white, lustrous jewel

_____ 6. to plunder a house

_____ 7. mild, or merciful; lenient

_____ 8. a small oval fruit, often used as a relish

_____ 9. to bully; to torment

_____ 10. a stick, or wand, or staff

_____ 11. a song or hymn

_____ 12. a stack of hay or straw

_____ 13. candid; outspoken

_____ 14. an opaque, highly colored kind of quartz

_____ 15. skill in performance; a knack

_____ 16. a short crowbar used by criminals

_____ 17. a pin of wood used to hang things on

_____ 18. the power of choosing one's own actions

_____ 19. light brown color

---------------- 20. a durable twilled cotton fabric

---------------- 21. to spread out for drying, especially hay

---------------- 22. a narrow beam of light; also a flat fish

---------------- 23. a standard or pattern

---------------- 24. a place where rabbits breed

---------------- 25. a British nobleman just above a viscount

(Notice what a rich source this is for possible punning!)

IV. Family Names

1. Read the chapter "Proper Names in America" in H. L. Mencken's *The American Language*. It includes fascinating information about name changes—the process and the reasons.
2. Check name endings (or beginnings) that indicate relationship in various languages, e.g., the suffix "son," the prefix "Mac," etc.
3. Glance at your local telephone directory and list five names that run to one column or more. (Nationally the most popular is Smith, with Johnson, Brown, Williams, Jones, and Miller as close contenders.)

Names are fascinating. An interest in names can be a fine springboard for developing sensitivity to words and word meaning.

16. WHAT'S IN A NAME? (Part 2)

Place-names are fascinating, too. *If* we become actively aware of them, they can tell us many things—the historical past, the prevailing national origin, the social and political attitudes, even the religious affiliations, past or present. But this knowledge becomes real knowledge only *if* we make ourselves aware of place-names. Too often we use them only to give directions.

I. Street Names

Take a quick survey of the names of streets in your town or city. Which streets, if any, were named after local heroes and events? Note the frequent use of names of flowers, trees, famous men, and numbers. Why do cities favor numbers? Why do suburbs favor flowers and trees? Why does Washington, D.C., use for its streets the names of states? Why would most people rather live on Wisteria Place than on Weed Street?

II. City Names

A. Start, of course, by investigating the name of the city or town in which you live. It is amazing how many people are totally ignorant of the meaning of the name or the reason for its choice.

B. Turn to the geographical section of a dictionary or to an atlas. Become an explorer of place-names. Ask yourself provocative questions. Why do many small towns choose a name like Paris? Why do so many towns and cities use "New" as part of their names: New Bedford, New Haven, New Albany, etc.? Why do a few use "Old" as in Old Westbury, Old Orchard Beach? Why are so many California cities prefixed by "San" or "Santa"—San Bernardino, San Diego, Santa Clara? Why does a state like Florida have an unusual number of two-part names: Lake City, Miami Beach, Plant City, Winter Haven, Coral Gables? Compare the names of towns and cities in Wisconsin with those in Massachusetts. What differences are immediately evident? Can you explain these differences?

C. Many place-names have a separate dictionary meaning when not capitalized. Can you identify the place-names that will fit the following definitions? (All are names of towns and cities in the United States; the name of the state in which each is located is given in parentheses.)

> *Example:* a large rounded rock (Colorado)
> *Answer:* Boulder

-------------------- 1. a hard quartz that strikes fire with steel (Michigan)

-------------------- 2. a large upholstered sofa (Iowa)

-------------------- 3. a common citrus fruit (New Jersey)

-------------------- 4. a challenge; contempt for opposition (Ohio)

-------------------- 5. a hardwood tree with a sweet edible nut (North Carolina)

-------------------- 6. a hardy cereal grass (New York)

-------------------- 7. a manservant, often the head servant (Pennsylvania)

-------------------- 8. easily movable; changeable (Alabama)

----------------- 9. a legendary bird that lives 500 years, is consumed by fire, then rises from its own ashes (Arizona)

----------------- 10. dawn; the rising light of morning (Illinois)

----------------- 11. a signal fire or guiding light (New York)

----------------- 12. harmony; a state of agreement (New Hampshire)

----------------- 13. a monster, half-lion and half-eagle (Georgia)

----------------- 14. a treeless plain; an open, level area (Georgia)

----------------- 15. an isolated hill; a mount with steep sides (Montana)

III. Store Names

Query local store owners to find out why the stores are named as they are. In many cases, the reason is obvious: the Five-and-Ten; Brown's Pharmacy. But how about Wardell's Grocery, which is owned by Mr. Jackson, or the Atlas Roofing Company, or the T & T Deli? Is a store name important? Why might the owner or manager change the name of a store? At one time a large department store on Long Island tried to change its name to Love. The public refused to accept the new name; can you understand this? How much is a nationally known name worth, from a practical point of view? What are some store and restaurant names known throughout the country? What does each suggest?

By now, you should be more sensitive to names—their origins, their significance, their importance in our daily lives.

17. AN ECOLOGICAL CATECHISM*

The scene is Borneo. The huts of the villagers are buzzing with houseflies. But never fear! The gecko, a charming little lizard, is present and devours flies joyfully. He can't eradicate them, but he can keep them under control.

Enter the new hero: DDT. Miraculously, the houseflies die. The gecko keeps right on eating—flies and DDT. And dies. The housecat eats geckos—plus flies and DDT. And dies. With the cats away, the rats will play. And suddenly the plague, carried by rats, is a real and terrifying possibility.

This is not a fairy tale. It actually happened. It is a simple but graphic picture of what *can* happen when men play games with ecology.

Ecology is "the science of the relationships of living creatures with each other and with their environment." Less technically, it is a study of the way living things affect each other, the way they affect their environment, and the way their environment affects them. Just so, in the opening story, the entire chain—the flies, the gecko, the cat, the rat, and eventually the human—were affected when DDT was used against the flies.

Ecology is a science that, a few years ago, was known only to the specialists. Today it is of major importance to every thinking human being. Man's inventions and carelessness are causing ecological imbalances that threaten even the survival of the human race.

Can you identify the following ecological perils?

_____ 1. chemical substances for destroying mosquitoes, flies, etc.

_____ 2. cleansing materials, often containing enzymes and phosphates

_____ 3. a mixture of smoke and fog

_____ 4. chemical substances for destroying plants

_____ 5. radiation from the disintegration of an atomic nucleus

Each of the above endangers our ecological environment; therefore each endangers our very existence and the existence of our planet Earth.

Check your answers above before you proceed to the following "catechism." Read the questions and answers thoughtfully and note the underlined words. Be ready for an ecological quiz at the end.

1. Q. What is the biosphere?
   A. The biosphere is that portion of the earth extending from the deepest roots to the tops of the highest trees.

2. Q. What is our era sometimes called?
   A. The "biosphere self-destruct era."

3. Q. What are internal clocks?
   A. The still mysterious mechanisms within most creatures that govern their waking and sleeping, and sometimes their pulse and heart rates.

4. Q. How is man's internal clock being disturbed today?
   A. Jet planes travel through several time zones. These sudden time changes necessitate adjustments in the 24-hour schedule that disturb man's sense of time and cause psychological and physical pressures.

---

* Remember: a catechism is any question-and-answer book.

5. Q. What are pollutants?
   A. Substances that seriously contaminate air or water. Gas and smoke are common air pollutants; sewage is a major water pollutant.

6. Q. What is one method of fighting pollution?
   A. Antipollution ordinances, or laws, are being passed to control or at least diminish pollution.

7. Q. What is a person called who works to preserve open lands, wetlands, wild life, etc.?
   A. A conservationist.

8. Q. How do detergents affect ecology?
   A. They contain phosphates that stimulate plant growth. The plants then consume extra oxygen from the water, thus turning lakes prematurely dry.

9. Q. What is predator/prey interaction?
   A. The predator (for example, the hawk) gains nourishment from his prey (the snake). Snakes, as a group, gain also, since their numbers are controlled, preventing overpopulation and subsequent famine.

10. Q. What is a biodegradable material?
    A. A substance that can be broken down by a natural means (for example, by bacteria) and that will return to its natural components.

11. Q. How do "throwaways" (plastic cartons, no-deposit bottles, etc.) affect our ecological environment?
    A. Some throwaways are non-biodegradable, that is, they will not easily return to their natural components. Almost all can be used only once and cannot be recycled.

12. Q. What does recycled mean?
    A. Paper can be used, then sold and made into pulp paper. Anything that is reused or remade is thereby recycled.

Now, without turning back to the ecological catechism, fill the blanks in the following sentences by inserting ecological terms.

1. An ordinance is a(n) _____. An antipollution ordinance is a(n) _____ against _____.

2. The instinctive sense of time that governs our minds and bodies is called a(n) _____ _____.

3. The portion of the earth supporting life below the ground, on the ground, and above the ground is called the _____.

4. A person who works to save open lands and wild life is called a(n) _____.

5. A major air pollutant, a mixture of smoke and fog, is called _____.

6. Which substance in most detergents is drying up our lakes prematurely? _____.

7. Substances that can be broken down by bacteria into their natural components are called _____ substances.

8. Sewage is a major source of _____ _____.

9. Materials that can be reused or remade can be _____.

10. The science concerned with the relationship of living creatures with each other and with their

world is _ _ _ _ _ _ _ _ _ _ _ _ _ .

Francis Thompson, the poet, once wrote, "Thou canst not stir a flower without troubling of a star." Only now is science catching up with poetry; only now are we beginning to realize the truth in Thompson's words.

18. "OF SHOES—AND SHIPS—AND SEALING-WAX"

"The time has come," the Walrus said,
"To talk of many things:
Of shoes—and ships—and sealing-wax—
Of cabbages—and kings—
And why the sea is boiling hot—
And whether pigs have wings."

—Lewis Carroll (*Alice Through the Looking-Glass*)

In this passage, Lewis Carroll, humorist and lover of words, was listing topics of conversation not haphazardly, but categorically. "Shoes" stands for the clothing man wears; "ships" for the vehicles by which he moves about; "sealing-wax" for the miscellaneous objects that are part of his daily life.

For each of the three categories, there is below a list of definitions of words often related. Below each list of words is a group of ten sentences. By considering context, word clues, etc., try to match the definitions with the underlined words.

I. "Shoes"

a. many-colored		*f.* showy	
b. spicy; exciting		*g.* brilliant	
c. cheap; not durable		*h.* out of date	
d. large, roomy		*i.* spotted	
e. sheer		*j.* very strange, fantastic	

_ _ _ _ 1. The resplendent gowns on the dancers transformed the stage into a wonderland.

_ _ _ _ 2. As soon as she had bought the skirt, she knew she shouldn't have; the workmanship was poor and the material sleazy.

_ _ _ _ 3. When Bob walked into the room, we all stared in surprise at his variegated plaid suit.

_ _ _ _ 4. Lady Rockford's bizarre new hat won its owner a round of chuckles and guffaws.

_ _ _ _ 5. Her capacious skirt, with its four large pockets, was perfect for shoplifting—or so she thought.

_ _ _ _ 6. The white dress, flecked with blue and red, was more than appropriate for the Fourth of July parade.

_ _ _ _ 7. Her gossamer hose accentuated her newly acquired summer tan.

_ _ _ _ 8. Gwen's outfit—mink, diamonds, and golden slippers—was, to put it mildly, ostentatious.

_ _ _ _ 9. The tall red feather added a piquant touch to her otherwise somber costume.

_ _ _ _ 10. With the radical change in fashion, her entire wardrobe became obsolete.

II. "Ships"

a. silver	*f.* stubborn; difficult
b. old and worn out	*g.* mutilated; disabled
c. sober; calm	*h.* huge; immense
d. shrill; grating	*i.* immoderate; excessive
e. light; floatable	*j.* wandering

____ 1. The titanic ship dwarfed the small rowboat.

____ 2. Thanks to our refractory horse, which refused to cross the highway, we never did get to our destination.

____ 3. Our errant car seemed to have a mind of its own as it traced its way over narrow country roads.

____ 4. The decrepit auto just stopped. No matter what the driver did, his vehicle simply refused to move.

____ 5. The argent airplane, swooping through the sunlight, glittered like mica.

____ 6. The strident voice of the locomotive shattered the silence of the countryside.

____ 7. The motorboat, traveling at an inordinate speed, caused two rowboats and a canoe to capsize.

____ 8. The buoyant raft rode easily over the crests of the waves.

____ 9. The maimed jet waddled down the runway like a dazed duck.

____ 10. The spectators watched in stunned silence as the sedate sedan outdistanced the sleek racers.

III. "Sealing-Wax"

a. produced artificially	*f.* covered with transparent sheets
b. longer lasting	*g.* defamatory; false and malicious
c. self-acting and self-regulating	*h.* involved; complicated
d. noisy; difficult to control	*i.* made of fired and baked clay
e. much decorated; ornate	*j.* converted into stone

____ 1. My host was obviously proud of his expensive rococo furniture. I didn't tell him that I preferred the simple straight lines of modern furniture.

____ 2. We use as a paperweight a piece of petrified wood that we found in Arizona.

____ 3. Although I once preferred natural wools and cottons, I now select synthetic fabrics for certain uses.

____ 4. The best-selling novel, which destroyed both the doctor's reputation and his practice, was clearly libelous.

____ 5. The automatic air-conditioner turned itself on and off at regular intervals.

____ 6. The ceramic ashtray, which graced our coffee table, is the result of a month's hard work in a handicraft class.

____ 7. A well-made hammer is a better buy than a cheap hammer: for one thing, it is more durable.

101 Ways to Learn Vocabulary

---- 8. His diploma, lovingly <u>laminated</u>, hangs on the living room wall.

---- 9. The lazy susan, handpainted with an <u>intricate</u> pattern of forget-me-nots, was originally my grandmother's.

---- 10. Our lawn mower was as <u>obstreperous</u> as a rebellious child.

19. "OF CABBAGES—AND KINGS"

Without food, man could not survive. Without man, language would not exist. So two major categories of words are words that describe *cabbages* and *kings*, that is, food and man.

I. "Cabbages"

Here is a list of definitions for words related to food. Read the sentences carefully; by considering context, word clues, etc., try to match the definitions with the underlined words.

a. juicy	*f.* lavish, magnificent
b. smelling of stale fat	*g.* pertaining to the sense of taste
c. dulled	*h.* agreeable to the taste
d. lukewarm	*i.* drink
e. orange	*j.* shriveled

---- 1. The saffron icing was exactly right for the cupcakes for the Halloween party.

---- 2. He had already attended two dinners that evening. As he arrived at the third banquet, he admitted that his appetite was rather jaded.

---- 3. The orange was so succulent that Jim had to wash his face and hands after he had eaten it.

---- 4. I am no epicure, but I do insist on palatable food.

---- 5. It was the last apple of the season—small, wizened, and discolored.

---- 6. The butter in the frying pan must not have been fresh. As I walked into the kitchen, a rancid odor assailed me.

---- 7. If you imbibe too freely at a cocktail party, you will find yourself in no condition to drive.

---- 8. It was 10° below zero. I came home craving a hot drink. My wife served tepid tea. I almost divorced her.

---- 9. The appetizing aroma drifting in from the kitchen made him think of gustatory pleasures.

---- 10. Living alone, I was accustomed to meager dinners. Perhaps that's why the seven-course dinner seemed absolutely sumptuous.

II. "Kings"

Food is luscious, but people are more exciting. These exercises depend on your knowledge of people and of human nature.

A. Answer the following questions; state briefly the reason for each answer.

If you were an employer, would you hire

1. a *dilettante* for the lead of a Broadway show?

----

2. a *misanthrope* to do social work?

----

101 Ways to Learn Vocabulary

3. a *zealot* to act as your campaign manager?

----

4. a *tyro* to manage your business?

----

5. a *sycophant* to help you improve your writing?

B. Match the first and second columns so that each completed sentence will make sense.

---- 1. A somnambulist should   *a.* try to stimulate his students.

---- 2. A proxy should   *b.* learn to play solitaire.

---- 3. A charlatan should   *c.* vote as he is directed to.

---- 4. A pedagogue should   *d.* live with a light sleeper.

---- 5. A celibate should   *e.* fear the police, magistrates, and all wise men.

C. Below are five pairs of words. Insert each pair into one of the five sentences. Be careful to place the words in logical order.

flamboyant	parsimonious	discerning
plain	prodigal	obtuse
irascible	ingenuous	
good-natured	sophisticated	

1. Susan hates to spend money. She is ------------------------- rather than

-------------------------.

2. Gloria reminds me of a peacock. She is ------------------, not ------------------.

3. The young starlet was too naive for Hollywood society; she was --------------------,

not ----------------------------.

4. Mr. Brown's bad temper grew worse each year. By the time he was an old man, he was

------------------------- rather than -------------------------.

5. A brilliant and sensitive man, Judge Clark's comments were always ------------------,

never ----------------------.

D. Here is a list of definitions of words related to man and his actions. Study the sentences carefully; by considering context and word clues, try to match the definitions with the underlined words.

a. temperate, sparing   f. mysterious, obscure
b. aggressive   g. harsh, shrill
c. blameworthy   h. ghostly
d. proper   i. tasteless, dull
e. lethargic, dull   j. red, florid

---- 1. Her insipid conversation at times bored me and at other times annoyed me.

---- 2. Her teachers never had to reprimand her, much less chastise her: her behavior was always decorous.

---- 3. From the lieutenant's cryptic remarks, we couldn't tell if the police had found any clue. Obviously he was not going to tell us.

---- 4. When Geraldine refused a cocktail and hors d'oeuvres, her friends ridiculed her for her abstemious habits.

---- 5. As the seance progressed, we heard a spectral voice in the darkness—and shivered.

---- 6. His truculent attitude made him a good front-line soldier but a thoroughly unsatisfactory citizen.

---- 7. The day was hot and humid; the students were torpid and inattentive.

---- 8. Because of his rubicund complexion, Matt's friends considered him healthy, but his doctor knew it was the result of high blood pressure.

---- 9. His conduct was reprehensible. I could neither condone it nor pity him.

---- 10. My head aching, I resented more than ever the raucous cries of the crows.

20. IN SEARCH OF PRECISENESS

Examining related words in groups will help you not only to remember these words but also to develop preciseness in choice of words. In each group below study closely the words and the definitions; then match them. Work first with the words you know well. Next *think* about the others. Make use of prefixes and associated words whenever possible. Use the dictionary only as a last resort.

I. ____ 1. riddle

____ 2. conundrum

____ 3. puzzle

____ 4. dilemma

____ 5. problem

a. a question, problem, or toy that perplexes the mind and tests one's ingenuity

b. a situation presenting two undesirable alternatives

c. a deliberately obscure question whose answer can be arrived at by guessing

d. a question proposed for solution or discussion

e. a riddle that involves a pun, or play on words

II. ____ 1. book

____ 2. pamphlet

____ 3. brochure

____ 4. monograph

____ 5. periodical

a. a short work, sometimes controversial, on some subject; enclosed in paper covers

b. a treatise on a single subject

c. a publication issued at regular intervals

d. a pamphlet, especially one used to advertise a product or place

e. a printed work of some length

III. ____ 1. monument

____ 2. monolith

____ 3. obelisk

____ 4. dolmen

____ 5. stele

a. a structure made of two upright stones capped by a horizontal stone and thought to be a tomb

b. a pillar of stone bearing an inscription; often a burial stone

c. a single great stone

d. a stone or structure erected in memory of a person or event

e. a tapering, four-sided shaft of stone

IV. ____ 1. university

____ 2. college

____ 3. institute

____ 4. seminary

____ 5. academy

a. a school for instruction in a particular art or science, e.g., for military instruction

b. a school for the education of men for the priesthood or ministry

c. an institution of learning of the highest grade, including a liberal arts college, a graduate school, and professional schools

d. an independent institution *or* a unit of a university, usually one devoted to a specialized field, e.g., medicine

e. an institution, beyond the secondary school level, devoted to instruction in technical subjects

V. ____ 1. dictionary   *a.* a dictionary of geographical names

    ____ 2. gazetteer   *b.* a listing of the words of a language, arranged alphabetically, with meanings and other information

    ____ 3. glossary

    ____ 4. thesaurus   *c.* an alphabetical index of the principal words of a book with a reference to the passage in which each occurs

    ____ 5. concordance

d. a list, with definitions, of technical or difficult words used in a subject or in a book

e. a book of synonyms and related words

Part III. *Handling Words*

Knowing words is good; *handling* them is better. Like any raw material, words are useful and profitable only when they are arranged properly and put to work.

Continue the analogy. Words are like gold nuggets: interesting to look at, to feel, perhaps to "pocket" like souvenirs. But when the gold is extracted from the nugget, when it is "handled" and made into a gold ring or a gold cup, then it has new meaning and acquires, in a sense, a new life. So with words. Simply *as* words, they are entertaining, fascinating, and exciting. When "handled" properly, they become the elements from which beautiful objects are created.

How does one handle words?

In several ways:

1. By discriminating choice. Choosing the right word at the right time is the first step.
2. By skillful phrasing. Combining words rhythmically and memorably is an art—an art that everyone could use.
3. By emphasizing words through word order. There *is* a difference between "beauty in the eye of the beholder" and "beauty in the beholder's eye" and "in the beholder's eye, beauty."

The result? The important result is that you will be more effective in expressing yourself and your ideas. No longer will you find yourself floundering in embarrassment, as you mutter, "I know what I mean, but I can't say it!"

1. POINT OF VIEW

Words that are similar in meaning may be miles apart in their effect because of the connotations they carry. Hence, *your* son is *rash*, but *my* son is *adventurous*; *your* house is a *mess*, but *my* house is *lived-in*. The situation or condition described may be identical, but the point of view is different.

Show contrasting points of view by completing the following list. Choose words that have a favorable connotation.

1. You are stubborn, but I am _____.

2. You are mediocre, but I am _____.

3. You are parsimonious, but I am _____.

4. You are gullible, but I am _____.

5. You are overbearing, but I am _____.

6. You are childish, but I am _____.

7. You are abrupt, but I am _____.

8. You are sanctimonious, but I am _____.

9. You are closemouthed, but I am _____.

10. You are submissive, but I am _____.

11. You are arrogant, but I am _____.

12. You are apathetic, but I am _____.

13. You are meddlesome, but I am _____.

14. You are unchangeable, but I am _____.

15. You are peculiar, but I am _____.

16. You are reckless, but I am _____.

17. You are shrewd, but I am _____.

18. You are slow, but I am _____.

19. You are talkative, but I am _____.

20. You are timid, but I am _____.

Follow-up: After you have completed the sentences, consider the very different connotations of the two words in each pair. Discriminating consideration of these pairs will help you to see the importance of exact word choice and will provoke some interesting ideas about the idiosyncrasies of human nature.

2. WORDS THAT EDITORIALIZE

Not every newspaper editorializes* outside of its editorial columns, but an increasing number do. A carefully focused study of a newspaper can alert you to the very real power of words. You will discover that forceful expression depends on one major factor: a writer's choice of words. There is a difference between the headline "City Officials Accused of Graft" and the headline "City Council Riddled by Graft?" The use of "City Council" suggests widespread rot; the use of "riddled" suggests both abundance and the violence associated with machine guns. Which headline does a newspaper use? If it politically favors the City Council or follows a conservative policy, it will use the first; if it is politically opposed to the City Council or pursues sensationalism, it will use the second.

A study of word-editorializing can be approached in several ways:

I. Through headlines

A. Compare the two following headlines:

<table>
<tr><td align="center">Air Traffic Controllers
Continue Slowdown</td><td align="center">Air Traffic Controllers
Mock Passenger Peril</td></tr>
</table>

Both headlines cover the same basic story; the second one is obviously editorializing, but the first is not. In the second headline, which two words do the editorializing?

1. _____   2. _____

B. *Sports Item:* Last Saturday the Allen High School football team defeated the York High School football team with a score of 14–13.

  Headline: **Allen Trounces York**

  1. Which school paper, Allen's or York's, would be most likely to use the above headline?

  _____

  2. What does the word *trounce* mean? _____

  3. What does *trounce* really mean in this headline? _____

C. Consider this headline:

28 G.I.'s Massacred
In Ruthless Ambush

  1. What effect does the use of the abbreviation *G.I.'s* have when used instead of the expression *American soldiers*?

  _____

  _____

---

* If you express an opinion, directly or indirectly, in a report that is supposed to be objective, you are *editorializing*.

2. If *killed* was substituted for *massacred*, what change in meaning would result?

----

3. What does the word *ruthless* mean? ------------------------------
Why is it used here?

II. Through stories

A. Below are two versions of the same news story. Read both of them.

1.   Eleanor Forrest, sixteen-year-old daughter of John L. Forrest, disappeared from her home three days ago. Miss Forrest left no note, but she did take a suitcase and some clothing. According to her distraught parents, the girl had about fifteen dollars when she left. Last night Mr. Forrest asked the police for assistance in tracing his daughter.

   Mr. Forrest is a candidate for County Commissioner. He is scheduled to speak tonight at a Youth in Politics meeting and expects to be there, noting that while there was little he could do at the moment for his daughter, there might be much he could do to inform other young people of their political rights and responsibilities.

2.   Last night several detectives talked to John L. Forrest, a candidate for County Commissioner, about the sudden and unexplained disappearance of his sixteen-year-old daughter Ellie. Ellie dropped out of sight three days ago. In her closet are dozens of pretty dresses and a shoerack holding nine pairs of pumps and loafers. The girl's bank account was not touched; nor was the "piggy bank," actually a weeping clown, in which she has collected pennies and nickels since she was a little girl.

   Today the Forrest home is a restless, unhappy place. A friend of the missing girl whispered something about a quarrel between Ellie and her father. Ellie's ten-year-old brother Tim is lonely, and Mrs. Forrest's eyes are red from weeping. Mr. Forrest is scheduled to speak tonight at a political rally. When asked if he would keep the engagement, Mr. Forrest said emotionlessly: "Of course I'll keep it. There is no reason not to."

a. Which facts are emphasized in each newspaper story?

----

101 Ways to Learn Vocabulary

b. How does the word choice in newspaper #2 differ from the word choice in newspaper #1?

----

c. How does the length of each story affect the impact on the reader?

----

d. What is the underlying purpose apparent in each version?

B. Now here are some facts concerning an automobile accident. Write the story twice—once in a straight style with no attempt to influence opinion, and once in a sensational style.

Time: January 1, at 2 a.m.

Place: on First Street, at the intersection with Vine Boulevard.

Accident: Automobile #1, a red Buick convertible, and automobile #2, a black jalopy, collided. Automobile #1 was driven by Roy Hawkins, a 38-year-old businessman. Automobile #2 was driven by James McKeller, an 18-year-old high school drop-out. Police asked both men to agree to an alcohol test. They are questioning both. Mr. Hawkins has a broken leg and lacerations on his face. Mr. McKeller was not hurt.

- -
- -
- -
- -
- -
- -
- -
- -
- -
- -
- -

Follow up by noticing, as you read a newspaper story, if it is slanted, how words are *used*, how ideas are *implied* rather than stated. Become aware—and you will soon realize that there is as much art in *reading* a newspaper story as in *writing* one!

3. DEFT DEFINITIONS

Daffy definitions have been around for a long time; so have deft definitions. But the deft definition has an advantage: it is truer, deeper, more thought-provoking than even a dictionary definition. Each of the following deft definitions was written by a skilled author and/or philosopher. Consider these definitions carefully. Then try to match each of the words below with a definition. You may find that you are a better philosopher than you think!

avarice	experience	laughter	population
culture	faith	liberty	remorse
economy	fear	love	science
education	hope	patience	war
evolution	knowledge	peace	work

1. _____ is nothing else but sudden glory arising from some sudden conception of some eminency in ourselves, by comparison with the infirmity of others, or with our own formerly.—Thomas Hobbes

2. _____ is going without something you do want in case you should, some day, want something you probably won't want.—Anthony Hope

3. _____ is the wisdom of the fool and the folly of the wise.—Samuel Johnson

4. I like _____; it fascinates me. I can sit and look at it for hours. I love to keep it by me: the idea of getting rid of it nearly breaks my heart.—Jerome K. Jerome

5. _____, when unchecked, increases in geometrical ratio. Subsistence only increases in an arithmetical ratio.—Thomas Malthus

6. _____, the beggar's virtue.—Philip Massinger

7. _____ enormous makes a God of me.—John Keats

8. _____ is nothing but trained and organized common sense.—Thomas Huxley.

9. _____ means responsibility. That is why most men dread it.—George Bernard Shaw

10. _____ makes people easy to lead, but difficult to drive; easy to govern, but impossible to enslave.—Baron Brougham

11. _____ is a good breakfast, but it is a bad supper.—Francis Bacon

12. A _____ is of the nature of a conquest;
For then both parties nobly are subdu'd,
And neither party loses.

—William Shakespeare

13. _____, the acquainting ourselves with the best that has been known and said in the world, and thus with the history of the human spirit.—Matthew Arnold

14. _____ is the substance of things hoped for, the evidence of things not seen.
—St. Paul

15. _____ is a change from an indefinite, incoherent homogeneity, to a definite, coherent heterogeneity.—Herbert Spencer

16. _____ is the parent of cruelty.—James Froude

17. If men could learn from history, what lessons it might teach us! But passion and party blind our

    eyes, and the light which _____ gives is a lantern on the stern, which shines

    only on the waves behind us!—Samuel Coleridge

18. _____ is much too serious a thing to be left to military men.—Talleyrand

19. _____, the fatal egg by pleasure laid.—William Cowper

20. _____, the spur of industry.—David Hume

Follow-up: Don't miss this opportunity to sharpen your analytical skills. Ask yourself *why* fear
is the parent of cruelty (#16), in what sense patience is a beggar's virtue (#6), what definition #3 tells
us about the effects of love. Ask yourself, too, why a "deft" definition is more effective and more
memorable than a dictionary definition.

4. A WIT FOR WRITING

Here is a "game" that can be played at any time and that will help you to appreciate the need for choosing exactly the right word. Test your wits against the leading writers of all times. Can you find exactly the right expression to complete each of the following quotations? If you are "stymied" by any one of the quotations, you can select the correct expression from the list below.

laps	smiled	conquering	disputed
No matter	luxuries	ballot	disdains
gash	swallows	innovate	feel
indifferent	decked	bud	frozen
refute	damp	brawls	toddle

1. Give us the _____ of life, and we will dispense with its necessities. —Oliver Wendell Holmes

2. See, the _____ hero comes!
Sound the trumpets, beat the drums!
                              —Thomas Morell

3. As though a rose should shut, and be a _____ again.—John Keats

4. They'll take suggestion as a cat _____ milk.—William Shakespeare

5. The world is a comedy to those that think, a tragedy to those that _____.
—Horace Walpole

6. Whatever _____ disturb the street,
There should be peace at home.
                              —Isaac Watts

7. A night-cap _____ his brows instead of bay;
A cap by night—a stocking all the day!
                              —Oliver Goldsmith

8. A noble mind _____ to hide his head,
And let his foes triumph in his overthrow.
                              —Robert Greene

9. The universe is not hostile, nor yet is it friendly. It is simply _____.
—John Haynes Holmes

10. The _____ is stronger than the bullet.—Abraham **Lincoln**

11. And hence some master-passion in the breast,

Like Aaron's serpent, _____ up the rest.
                              —Alexander Pope

12. What is Matter?—Never mind.

What is Mind? _____
                              —*Punch*

13. And when the war is done and youth stone dead

I'd _____ safely home and die—in bed.
                              —Siegfried Sassoon

14. Architecture in general is _____ music.—Friedrich Von Schelling

15. I have a rendezvous with Death

    At some _____ barricade.

    > —Alan Seeger

16. Cervantes _____ Spain's chivalry away.—Lord Byron

17. To _____ is not to reform.—Edmund Burke

18. A castle, precipice-encurled,

    In a _____ of the wind-grieved Apennine.

    > —Robert Browning

19. I am aware of the _____ souls of housemaids
    Sprouting despondently at area gates.

    > —T. S. Eliot

20. Who can _____ a sneer?—Rev. William Paley

Follow-up: After you have checked your answers, don't stop. Use Socratic questioning on yourself to see if you know *why* the right word is the right word. What does Eliot mean by "damp souls" (#19)? Why is "damp" a successful word choice in this context? Why is "ballot" so effective in #10? What unusual break in mood is caused by "toddle" in #13? In #18, why is "gash" appropriate so soon after "precipice-encurled"? Why is the thought in #17 especially provocative today? Could this expression be more succinct than it is?

5. SENSITIZING THE SENSES

Before you begin this exercise, in the space below write a brief paragraph describing a steak dinner, a diamond necklace, or a new car (or anything else you wish).

Now read the description you just wrote. Then answer these questions.

1. Did you use any words that relate to the sense of sight? Check "Yes" or "No."

   Yes ____ No ____ If yes, which ones? _____

2. Did you use any words that relate to the sense of hearing?

   Yes ____ No ____ If yes, which ones? _____

3. Did you use any words that relate to the sense of touch?

   Yes ____ No ____ If yes, which ones? _____

4. Did you use any words that relate to the sense of smell?

   Yes ____ No ____ If yes, which ones? _____

5. Did you use any words that relate to the sense of taste?

   Yes ____ No ____ If yes, which ones? _____

If you are like most people, you probably emphasized appearance and taste, and neglected almost completely the other three senses. But you have *five* senses—and the good writer involves all of them.

EYE WORDS

Here are some words, each relating to the way things *look*. Read the list slowly. Use a dictionary to investigate any unfamiliar words.

argent	tenebrous	glint	opalescent
cerulean	leaden	gloomy	pallid
luminous	rainbow	glow	pellucid
tawny	blaze	somber	radiant
sable	bleak	emerald	sparkle
murky	crepuscular	mosaic	tinsel
phosphorescent	diaphanous	iridescent	dingy
garish	flash	lucent	verdant
crystalline	glare	luster	dazzling
gaudy			

Ask yourself leading questions. What is the difference between *glare* and *glint*? Between *cerulean* and *blue*? Why use *sable* instead of *black*, or *rainbow* instead of *many-colored*? Remember that the use of the exactly right adjective will not only help you to paint a picture but will carry a connotation that will double the effectiveness of that picture.

EAR WORDS

Now go on to the second sense, hearing. Consider

clatter	roar	hubbub	trumpet
fanfare	pandemonium	hullabaloo	shrill
gurgle	babble	hiss	chime
jingle	wheeze	grate	twang
sonorous	clang	peal	alarm
bomb	thunder	bellow	resonant
silent	whistle	whisper	scream
cacophony	yelp	hush	lull
muteness	rustle	buzz	purr
moan	tinkle	clamorous	tintinnabulation
drone	whining	quaver	melodious
strident			

Again ask yourself questions. What is the difference between *clang* and *peal*? Between *hush* and *lull*? What would the word *pandemonium* exactly describe? The word *hubbub*? Why is so much modern music discordant? Why is the sitar suddenly a popular musical instrument? What is a friend's tone of voice like when he is happy? Angry? Annoyed? Hear!

TOUCH WORDS

As you approach the third sense, the sense of touch, you will have to put your imagination to work—unless you have easily available a collection of assorted objects. Imagine the *feel* of glossy paper, pulp paper, wallpaper, cellophane, aluminum foil; satin material, silk, velvet, corduroy, denim; a wood carving, a plastic statue, a small bronze; a piece of leather, a blotter, a sponge. Then think about words that graphically describe various "feels":

slimy	flabby	limp	velvet
smooth	downy	palpable	granular
rough	shaggy	scrape	satin
bumpy	powdery	oily	prickly
slippery	sandpaper	paw	manipulate
feathery	silk	rub	fluffy
hairy	corrugated	greasy	rumple
ooze	mossy	crisp	waxy
soft	pulpy	grope	jagged
textured	spiky	plush	scratch

As a follow-up, watch a toddler pick up a new object. The child caresses it, feeling its identity; rubs it against his cheek, feeling it in a different way; puts it in his mouth, feeling it with his tongue. He squeezes it, scratches it, bounces it as he *learns* the object. As we grow older, our sense of touch atrophies unless we deliberately foster it. Foster it.

NOSE WORDS

The fourth sense, the sense of smell, is most easily discussed if you are hungry. Think about the smells you have experienced lately and try to describe some. These suggestions may help:

aroma	musty	rank	whiff
bouquet	bergamot	redolent	odor
fetid	musk	reek	perfume
fragrant	pungent	scent	sachet
heady	putrid	spicy	foul
incense	rancid	stench	
garlic	skunk	cinnamon	

This is, in some respects, the most difficult sense to describe. It is the most nebulous, the least concrete.

TASTE WORDS

Finally, we come to the fifth sense—the sense of taste. Here is a list of words that can be used to describe taste:

syrup	delectable	flavor	palatable
caramel	vinegar	honey	briny
biting	luscious	saccharine	gamy
acerb	delicious	mustard	acrid
sour	ambrosial	tart	caustic
acid	gusto	insipid	nauseating
relish	savory	smack	tang
spicy	flat	mild	bland

When does *sweet* become *saccharine*? What is the difference between *sour* and *tart*? If we describe wine as *vinegary*, what do we mean? What are the several meanings of *relish*?

You are ready now for the conclusion. Write another paragraph, describing the same object depicted in the original paragraph. Involve *all* five senses if you possibly can. If this exercise has "taken," you should have an appetizing essay!

6. SENSE WITH SOUNDS

Some words are more than words; they are independent agents. Their sounds are so real, so true, that representation and reality seem to merge. A word like "buzz" not only *names* a sound; it *is* the sound. "Thump" is so vivid it almost hurts, and "crunch" starts the jaws working!

Only a few words are as independent as these, but many have achieved partial autonomy. Your appreciation of language—and your writing—will improve if you force your ears to become active partners with your brains.

Consider words that begin with "l"—*limp, laggard, lazy, limpid, loose, listless, languid*. Note the smooth, drawl-like quality of so many "l" words.

What about "b's"—*bomb, break, buck, bump, batter, burst, burp, bruise*? Do you hear the quick, forceful note, the result of exploding lips? Imagine "loose" spelled "boose" or "limp" as "bimp"!

"R"—this is a nice active letter. Only "r" could introduce *rattle, raid, rouse, riddle, rage, rant, rumble, ram*. Change "raid" to "maid," or "ram" to "ham"—can you hear the difference?

Then there's the slippery "s"—always elusive: *silver, swift, silent, sleep, sad, satin, sliver, slick*. Compare "burp" and "slurp," "rage" and "sage" to see the difference. The "sn's" demand a category all to themselves: *snap, snag, snip, snicker, sneer, snort, snarl, sneaky, snide, snake, snub*. Aren't they as nasty and unpleasant as words can be?

"M's" are smooth, but heavy, conducive to content: *murmur, meander, mercy, music, mull, mellow*—except when the heaviness erupts into violence: *murder, mayhem, mischief, monster, mangle*.

Don't forget vowel sounds, too. The open, emotion-packed, mellow sound to the long "o" or "oo" in *gold, told, moon, gloom*; the clipped, flippant sound of the short "i" in *tingle, flick, pit, flit, glitter, glimpse, mint*; the intense long "e" in *deep, scream, plead, teem, mean*.

Now see how sound-conscious *you* are. In the space below each question, write the answer that *sounds* right to you.

1. What do your ears tell you is the difference between *quiet* and *still*? Between *soft* and *downy*?

   ----

2. Read this stanza of Poe's "The Bells." Which sounds does Poe favor in writing about *silver* bells? Why?

> Hear the sledges with the bells,—
> Silver bells!
> What a world of merriment their melody foretells!
> How they tinkle, tinkle, tinkle,
> In the icy air of night!
> While the stars that oversprinkle
> All the heavens, seem to twinkle
> With a crystalline delight;
> Keeping time, time, time,
> In a sort of Runic rhyme,
> To the tintinnabulation that so musically wells
> From the bells, bells, bells, bells,
> Bells, bells, bells,—
> From the jingling and the tinkling of the bells.

----

3. If you wish to be very emphatic, would you choose a short word or a long word? If you are annoyed beyond endurance by a garrulous friend, will you tell him to "be silent" or to "shut up"? Why?

----

4. How do we make words "child-size"? How do we make them easy for two-year-olds? Doesn't a *cat* become a *kitty*, and a *pig*, a *piggy*? What does the final "e" sound contribute? It makes the word longer. Does this make sense?

----

5. Which kind of word would you use if you were writing a popular song—words with Old English (OE) or Latin (L) roots? Would you sing of *love* (OE) or *affection* (L)? Of *house* (OE) or *residence* (L)? Which kind of word is more often used in scholarly dissertations and in government instructions? Why?

----

6. Consider some popular slogans: "A call to arms!" "Keep the faith!" "Blood, sweat, and tears!" What do these slogans have in common? Do they use long or short words? Do the words have a "sound" meaning as well as a dictionary meaning? Do they connote as well as denote?

----

7. James Thurber once wrote that you can put yourself to sleep by listing, mentally, all the words you can think of that begin with one letter. He warned against "m" because of its latent violence! Try this some night. Does it help or hinder sleep? *Do* the words that begin with a specific letter often have something in common?

You may, in the future, suffer from insomnia, but when you do finally sleep, you can babble (in b's) or mutter (in m's). "He who has ears, let him hear!"

7. TRY A TRANSLATION!

Attempting to translate can be one method of making you aware of the importance of words. As you struggle with the translation, you will see the need for a large vocabulary so that you can choose the exact word for meaning and mood. As you struggle with word order, you will discover that words cannot be dropped haphazardly—that a particular word order is appropriate in a certain context.

Procedure:

1. Read, even if you do not understand it, the French poem "Le Mousse."
2. Now turn to the French-English glossary. First try a literal translation—a word-for-word translation.
3. Read the literal translation several times. Be sure you understand (*a*) what the poem says and (*b*) the mood of the poem.
4. Next try a poetic translation. Look for words that will emphasize the mood of the poem. Look for the word order that will provide a rhythmical flow.
5. Finally, read Dudley Fitts' translation. Compare it to *your* translation. Which is more effective? Why?

LE MOUSSE

—Mousse: il est donc marin, ton père? . . .
—Pêcheur. Perdu depuis longtemps.
En découchant d'avec ma mère,
Il a couché dans les brisants. . . .

Maman lui garde au cimetière
Une tombe—et rien dedans.—
C'est moi son mari sur la terre,
Pour gagner du pain aux enfants.

Deux petits.—Alors, sur la plage,
Rien n'est revenu du naufrage? . . .
—Son garde-pipe et son sabot. . .

La mère pleure, le dimanche,
Pour repos . . . Moi: j'ai ma revanche
Quand je serai grand—matelot!—
—Tristan Corbière

French-English Glossary

a, has
ai, have
alors, then, at that time
aux, to the, for the
avec, with

brisants, breakers

ce, this, that
cimetière, cemetery, churchyard
couché, goes to bed

dans, in, into, within
de, of, off, from
découchant, leave one's bed
dedans, inside, within
depuis, from, since
deux, two
dimanche, Sunday
donc, then, therefore
du, of the, from the, some, any

en, in, into
enfants, children
est, is
et, and

gagner, to gain, to earn
garde, keeps, preserves, watches over
garde-pipe, pipe-case
grand, big, tall, great

il, he, it

je, I

la, the
le, les, the
longtemps, long, a long while
lui, for him, for her, for it

ma, my
maman, mama
mari, husband
marin, seaman, sailor
mère, mother
moi, I, me
mousse, cabin boy, shipboy

naufrage, shipwreck
n', not

pain, bread
pêcheur, fisherman
perdu, lost, wrecked
père, father
petits, little ones, young ones
plage, beach, strand
pleure, weeps, cries
pour, for, for the sake of

quand, when

repos, rest, quiet
revanche, revenge, retaliation
revenu, came back
rien, nothing

sabot, shoe
serai, will be
son, his, her, its
sur, on, upon, over, about

terre, earth, soil, land, world
tombe, tomb, grave
ton, your

une, a, an

Translation

CABIN-KID

Your old man's a sailor, I suppose? . . .
—A fisherman. A long time dead.
He left my mother's side one night,
And sleeps in the breakers now instead.

Up in the graveyard there's a tomb
Ma keeps for him—it's empty, though—
I'm all the husband that she has
To help her while the children grow.

Two little ones.—Nothing was found
Along the beach where he was drowned? . . .
—Only his pipe-case and a shoe . . .

When Sundays come, Mother can stop
And cry for rest . . . But when I grow up
I'll get revenge—a sailor too!
                        —Translation by Dudley Fitts

8. BE SPECIFIC!

Writing can be made more vivid and more effective by using specific words wherever possible. Instead of saying "I lost my hat," say "I lost my blue tam." With this in mind, rewrite the following sentences, replacing the underlined general words with specific words.

1. As I entered the garden, I saw two kinds of birds.

   ----

2. Flowers of many types surrounded me.

   ----

3. A book lay on the coffee table.

   ----

4. She wore her new coat to school.

   ----

5. She loved the sound of the ocean.

   ----

6. The little boy climbed the tree in the backyard.

   ----

7. They spent the holiday on Frank Archer's boat.

   ----

8. For Christmas she received clothing and cosmetics.

   ----

9. His workbench was covered with tools.

   ----

10. In preparation for their camping trip, they filled a carton with food.

    ----

11. On the way to the river he tripped over something in the dark.

    ----

12. He went to the store for bread.

    ----

13. As he stepped heavily on her shoe, she tried unsuccessfully to smile.

    ----

14. The audience listened eagerly to their favorite music.

    ----

15. Her purse was filled with <u>many things</u>.

----

16. He watches <u>two types of shows</u> on television every night.

----

17. As the <u>plane flew</u> over the house, the baby began to cry.

----

18. Because he <u>was ill</u>, he could not go to the game.

----

19. The <u>dog</u> whined as the family car pulled away from the house.

----

20. After studying for <u>a long time</u>, I was ready for a <u>snack</u>.

----

9. BE SELECTIVELY SPECIFIC!

Sometimes being specific is not enough. You must be selectively specific. In a previous lesson, the sentence "As I entered the garden, I saw two kinds of birds" could be changed to "As I entered the garden, I saw robins and starlings." This is a definite improvement, but suppose you were writing a story of conflict and anger. Mightn't it be more effective to write "As I entered the garden, I saw a blackbird and a blue jay fighting over a bit of bread"? Or suppose your story took place in an exotic garden in the tropics. Wouldn't you then expect to see macaws and flamingos instead of robins and starlings?

Now replace the italicized word or words in each sentence below in accordance with the suggestions:

1. *A book* lay on the coffee table.

    --- *a.* to suggest wealth

    --- *b.* to suggest scholarship

2. In preparation for their camping trip, they filled a carton with *food*.

    --- *a.* if they were Boy Scouts

    --- *b.* if they were wealthy businessmen

3. He loved the *sound* of the ocean.

    --- *a.* on a quiet summer night

    --- *b.* on a stormy winter night

4. He entered the *house* at exactly 7 p.m.

    --- *a.* the home of a millionaire

    --- *b.* the home of a tramp

5. When he turned his head to the right, he saw *wild animals*.

    --- *a.* in the Far North

    --- *b.* in the jungle

6. He dropped his *clothes* on the floor and headed for the shower.

    --- *a.* after a day's work

    --- *b.* after a dance

7. When he saw the *car* in the driveway, he knew how many sales his rival had made.

    --- *a.* a great many sales

    --- *b.* very few sales

8. She bought a *toy* for her nephew.

    --- *a.* a three-year-old

    --- *b.* a twelve-year-old

9. Mrs. Jones bought three yards of *material*.

--- *a.* to cover a chair

--- *b.* to make a dress

10. I prefer this house because it is surrounded by *trees*.

--- *a.* in New York

--- *b.* in Florida

10. GOBBLEDEGOOK

Gobbledegook is language characterized by wordiness, indirectness, and, at times, excessive use of technical terms. The term gobbledegook was first used to describe the language used in government bulletins, announcements, etc. Today it exists in government reports, business memos, and educational and sociological publications. In fact, it is more prevalent than it was.

Translating gobbledegook into concise English and translating concise English into gobbledegook can be a challenging experience. Follow Steps I, II, and III, and you will become an expert in gobbledegook!

Step I. Begin by reading a couple of well-known examples of gobbledegook and their translations:

1. "Objective consideration of contemporary phenomena compels the conclusion that success or failure in competitive activities exhibits no tendency to be commensurate with innate capacity, but that a considerable element of the unpredictable must be taken into account."

   This is George Orwell's translation, in "Politics and the English Language," into gobbledegook of the following passage from Ecclesiastes: "I returned and saw under the sun, that the race is not to the swift, nor the battle to the strong, neither yet bread to the wise, nor yet riches to men of understanding, nor yet favor to men of skill; but time and chance happeneth to them all."

2. A veteran wrote to the government asking about a pension. He received the following answer:

   "The noncompensable evaluation heretofore assigned to you for your service-connected disability is confirmed and continued." (quoted in *Time*, May 7, 1947)

   It means, simply, that the veteran is not going to get a pension!

Step II. Here are four examples of gobbledegook versions of well-known proverbs. With the help of the dictionary, try to find the original proverbs.

1. It is an accepted fact that, in most cases, a male descendant will emulate, at least to some degree, his immediate male parent.

   ----

2. In the event of a minor mishap or accident, especially of an article of apparel or of related material, both intelligence and prudence suggest that an infinitesimal amount of thread can prevent the necessity of a much larger outlay of both material and effort.

   ----

3. Warm-blooded vertebrates of the class *Aves* that share an epidermal covering commonly known as plumage have a propensity for assembling, or perhaps one should say for congregating, in isolated and homogeneous crowds.

   ----

4. If one desires to become thoroughly cognizant of the character, meritorious or meretricious, of a specific individual, one should study, analyze, and evaluate those other individuals—business associates or social acquaintances—with whom the aforesaid specific individual generally, or even usually, prefers to spend his time.

Step III. You are almost an expert. Now test yourself by turning the following proverbs into gobbledegook.

1. A rolling stone gathers no moss.

----

2. Three can keep a secret when two of them are dead.

----

3. Haste makes waste.

----

4. Absence makes the heart grow fonder.

----

5. Out of sight, out of mind.

----

6. A penny saved is a penny earned.

A Word of Warning: Writing gobbledegook will extend your vocabulary and enhance your skill with words, but remember that the main purpose for writing is to communicate. Much gobbledegook fails to communicate. Hence, it is *not* good writing!

11. CONCERNING CLICHÉS

A *cliché* is a trite, stereotyped expression. Most clichés were effective when they were created, but overuse has exhausted them. They are now pale images indeed!

Step I. Begin with a review of color clichés. Read the first part, e.g., "as red as," and then jot down the first word or words that come to mind—in this case, probably "a rose." *Don't try to be imaginative!*

1. as brown as . . . ----------------------------------
2. as white as . . . ----------------------------------
3. as green as . . . ----------------------------------
4. as black as . . . ----------------------------------
5. as blue as . . . ----------------------------------

    Continue the clichés with some contrasting pairs:

6. as cool as . . . ----------------------------------
   as hot as . . . ----------------------------------
7. as pretty as . . . ----------------------------------
   as ugly as . . . ----------------------------------
8. as rich as . . . ----------------------------------
   as poor as . . . ----------------------------------
9. as fit as . . . ----------------------------------
   as sick as . . . ----------------------------------
10. as wise as . . . ----------------------------------
   as smart as . . . ----------------------------------
   as dumb as . . . ----------------------------------

    Continue with miscellaneous clichés.

11. as tight as . . . ----------------------------
12. to work like . . . ----------------------------
13. as high as . . . ----------------------------
14. as hard as . . . ----------------------------
15. as weak as . . . ----------------------------
16. as strong as . . . ----------------------------
17. as sly as . . . ----------------------------
18. as busy as . . . ----------------------------
19. as big as . . . ----------------------------
20. as sweet as . . . ----------------------------

21. as bitter as . . .   ---------------------

22. as happy as . . .   ---------------------

23. as smooth as . . .   ---------------------

24. cried like . . .   ---------------------

25. as clear as . . .   ---------------------

26. as clean as . . .   ---------------------

27. as quiet as . . .   ---------------------

28. slept like . . .   ---------------------

29. climbs like . . .   ---------------------

30. sadder but . . .   ---------------------

There can no longer be any doubt about what a cliché is! Go on to Step II.

Step II. Now is the time to put your imagination to work! Choose any ten of the above clichés and rewrite them to make the comparison fresh and meaningful. In each case the conclusion should *seem* inevitable with regard to rhythm and meaning, but should be original enough to carry an emotional impact and strange enough to startle the listener into deliberate appreciation of the image.

> *Example:*
> *Cliché:*   as bitter as gall
> *Revision:*   as bitter as a benched ballplayer

Now choose *your* ten and go to work!

1. Cliché: _____

   Revision: _____

2. Cliché: _____

   Revision: _____

3. Cliché: _____

   Revision: _____

4. Cliché: _____

   Revision: _____

5. Cliché: _____

   Revision: _____

6. Cliché: _____

   Revision: _____

7. Cliché: _____

   Revision: _____

8. Cliché: _____

   Revision: _____

9. Cliché: _____

   Revision: _____

10. Cliché: _____

    Revision: _____

12. FUN WITH PUNS

A pun is a play on words, or, to be more pedantic, "the humorous use of a word in such a manner as to bring out different meanings or applications, or of words alike or nearly alike in sound, but different in meaning." A pun is humor at its best and at its worst. It elicits more groans than any other form of humor, but it is cherished (derisively) by the intellectually perceptive and receptive.

Adam, the first man, figured in one of the earliest puns because he was named after the earth, *adamah*. And Jacob was appropriately named Jacob (meaning heel) because he came from the womb holding Esau's heel; but he was a heel, by the standards of any age, when he usurped his brother's proper heritage! In the New Testament when Christ said, "Thou art Peter, and upon this rock I will build my Church," he created one of the most far-reaching puns of all time; for Peter means "rock" and on this pun (to an extent) rests the founding of the Christian Church.

Shakespeare was a master of the pun. In *Julius Caesar* the cobbler calls himself, in safe conscience, "a mender of bad soles" (I,i,15), and later says, "I meddle with no tradesman's matters, nor women's matters, but with awl" (I,i,26).

Perhaps the most astonishing pun is the one attributed to the English poet Thomas Hood in the last moments of his life. He supposedly said, "Now the undertaker will earn (that is, *urn*) a livelihood (i.e., *lively Hood*)."

Punning can be both valuable and entertaining. It teaches us the connotation as well as the denotation of words. It sharpens our listening and heightens our perception. It makes us drunk with words. It emphasizes the stabbing, glittering quality of skillful word usage. Why not employ this much-maligned device in *your* conversation and writing?

But before you can become an expert, you must begin at the beginning—create some puns of your own. To help you, we have classified the pun by its several types.

I. First is the Pun Simple, based on homonyms. (Homonyms, remember, are words that *sound* alike but differ in spelling and meaning.) Shakespeare's pun with *awl* and *all*, and Hood's with *earn* and *urn* are excellent examples of this type. They're the easiest (though not easy!) to create, so begin with a few of these.

Suppose you take the pair of words *reign* and *rain*. Play with them. Think about their meanings. Manipulate them. Play one meaning against another. You may come up with something like this:

After the glorious years of Elizabeth I, the reign of King James was barely a drizzle.

Here are some sets that lend themselves to punning:

write-right-rite	plain-plane
stare-stair	none-nun
cache-cash	know-no
holy-wholly	mean-mien
freeze-frieze	sweet-suite

Choose two sets from the above suggestions and see if you can become a punster!

1. Words: _____

   Pun: _____

2. Words: _____

   Pun: _____

II. Second is the Bare Pun; it is the illegitimate offspring of the Pun Simple. This pun is based on a single word that has multiple meanings. Especially useful for this type of pun is the word that can act as a proper first name but that also has a separate dictionary meaning. Consider the word *will*. Suppose a friend named Will is discouraged. He cannot solve a problem he has been working on. You turn to him encouragingly and say, "Where there's a Will, there's a way!"

Here are some suggestions for the Bare Pun:

may	rob
frank	mark
prudence	pearl
rod	victor
art	ray

Again choose two—then pun!

1. Word: _____

   Pun: _____

2. Word: _____

   Pun: _____

Of course, the Bare Pun is not limited to proper nouns. Again Thomas Hood is the virtuoso. Note his use of *arms* in this next pun, remembering *arms* of a body and fire*arms*.

> Ben Battle was a soldier bold,
> And used to war's alarms:
> But a cannon-ball took off his legs,
> So he laid down his arms!

Here are suggested words for Bare Pun II. (Check the dictionary for multiple meanings when necessary.)

face	head
pine	hose
bridge	pants
lark	needle

1. Word: _____

   Pun: _____

2. Word: _____

   Pun: _____

III. Third is the Pun Complex. With this type you begin with a well-known phrase or proverb, then twist one or two words to fit the person or occasion. One fine example was concocted by George Oppenheimer, the drama critic. He described Dr. Timothy Leary as "a drugged individualist"!

Let's start with the best-known proverb of all, "A stitch in time saves nine." Say it out loud a few times. Listen to it. Manipulate the words. Then provide a setting. For example:

> An undertaker, thinking of a casket and noticing something odd about a "corpse" in his establishment, remarked, "A twitch in time saves pine."

Dreadful, isn't it? Now you try! Choose one phrase from Group 1 and change a word or two to create a Pun Complex! Then choose one expression in Group 2 and do the same.

GROUP 1

a barefoot boy
a raving maniac
an old-maid schoolteacher
an absent-minded professor

GROUP 2

A penny saved is a penny earned.
My country, right or wrong.
You can't teach an old dog new tricks.
Out of sight, out of mind.
It is better to be sure than sorry.
Spare the rod and spoil the child.

Are you game?

1. Words: _____

   Pun: _____

2. Words: _____

   Pun: _____

IV. Fourth is the Pun Perplexed. This is the aristocratic uncle of the family—a monocled, silver-haired gentleman burdened by degrees. A familiarity with allusions and a wide reading background are essential for understanding this rare bird!

George Kaufman, the playwright, once said, "One man's Mede is another man's Persian." This is double word-play, with a vengeance! It combines "One man's meat is another man's poison" with the Medes and Persians of the ancient world. The result is blatant in actuality but subtle in its allusive power.

No material is given this time. Draw on your entire stock of history and literature, your whole collection of proverbs and familiar sayings—then create!

_____

_____

13. "BRUSH UP YOUR SHAKESPEARE!"

Translating something that was written in the language of one era into the language of another can be an exhilarating experience . . . especially when the original was written by William Shakespeare! This type of translation emphasizes sense and mood, and gaily ignores actual words and word order. In addition, the "translator" may choose to modernize setting and types of characters. The result is always fascinating, though (when done to the Bard) horrifying, also, to lovers of Shakespeare!

Yet Shakespeare is the logical subject of this kind of exercise. When he speaks, he speaks of universals. His ideas are as relevant today as they were in 1600. But his language *is* different. Updating him will make you conscious of his language and aware of the strengths and defects of our modern idiom.

Begin with a well-known scene. Read it carefully, be sure you understand exactly what the dramatist is saying, then shrug away inhibitions and "re-write"—for the 1970's!

Here is the most famous scene of all from *Romeo and Juliet*.

Romeo.   She speaks.
O speak again, bright angel, for thou art
As glorious to this night, being o'er my head,
As is a winged messenger of Heaven
Unto the white-upturned wond'ring eyes
Of mortals that fall back to gaze on him
When he bestrides the lazy puffing clouds
And sails upon the bosom of the air.

Juliet. O Romeo, Romeo, wherefore art thou Romeo?
Deny thy father and refuse thy name;
Or if thou wilt not, be but sworn my love
And I'll no longer be a Capulet.

Romeo. Shall I hear more or shall I speak at this?

Juliet. 'Tis but thy name that is my enemy,
Thou art thyself, though not a Montague.
What's Montague? it is nor hand nor foot
Nor arm nor face. O be some other name
Belonging to a man.
What's in a name? that which we call a rose
By any other word would smell as sweet.
So Romeo would, were he not Romeo call'd,
Retain that dear perfection which he owes
Without that title. Romeo, doff thy name,
And for thy name, which is no part of thee,
Take all myself.

Romeo.   I take thee at thy word.
Call me but Love and I'll be new baptiz'd,
Henceforth I never will be Romeo.

And *here* is a modern version of the same scene written by two teen-agers.

Jason. Lori, you are really the most dynamite
thing that has ever happened to me!

> *Lori.* Jason, don't live on family status. Don't listen to
> what your people are trying to tell you.
>
>   Deny the prejudices of your class, and I'll deny
> mine.
>   (Pause)
>
> *Jason.* Yeah. Go ahead.
>
> *Lori.*   We are not enemies.
> It's just our different social classes. But would our
> souls change if I were poor and you were wealthy?
>   We are both human beings—in every way.
> Equal in every way.
>
> *Jason.* Take me and I'll take you. And we will
> become as one, together.

Obviously a number of things have happened! The young lovers have changed from Romeo and Juliet to Jason and Lori. The feud that threatens to separate the lovers was originally between families; now it is between social classes. The language certainly has changed, and so—even more sharply— has the tone. Romeo's gentle "Shall I hear more or shall I speak at this?" becomes Jason's "Yeah. Go ahead." But the *idea*—that love can surmount all obstacles—remains.

You may find the new version (if you dislike it) brash and curt; or you may find it (if you like it) simple and direct. Either way the abyss of 350 years is evident—but so is the human bridge that spans the abyss.

Here is another famous Shakespearean selection—this time from *Hamlet*. See what you can do about updating it to make it "fit" the twentieth century. (The scene describes the advice given by Polonius, an old wise fool, to his son Laertes, as Laertes is preparing to go abroad.)

> *Polonius.*   . . . my blessing with thee!
> And these few precepts in thy memory
> Look thou character. Give thy thoughts no tongue,
> Nor any unproportion'd thought his act.
> Be thou familiar, but by no means vulgar;
> Those friends thou hast, and their adoption tried,
> Grapple them unto thy soul with hoops of steel;
> But do not dull thy palm with entertainment
> Of each new-hatch'd, unfledg'd comrade. Beware
> Of entrance to a quarrel, but, being in,
> Bear 't that th' opposed may beware of thee.
> Give every man thy ear, but few thy voice;
> Take each man's censure, but reserve thy judgment.
> Costly thy habit as thy purse can buy,
> But not express'd in fancy; rich, not gaudy;
> For the apparel oft proclaims the man,
> And they in France of the best rank and station
> Are of a most select and generous clef in that.
> Neither a borrower, nor a lender be;
> For loan oft loses both itself and friend,
> And borrowing dulleth edge of husbandry.
> This above all: to thine own self be true,

And it must follow, as the night the day,
Thou canst not then be false to any man.

Now—*your* version!

----

14. PORTRAIT PAINTING

Conjure up a picture of a close friend. Got it? Now suppose you were asked to describe him. What would you say? Write a brief description.

- -

- -

- -

- -

- -

Look again at what you wrote. You probably said that he has dark eyes, brown hair, a big nose, and is kind of tall—or something similar. That's how most people describe someone. But is this description effective? Does it "capture" your friend? Does it tell anyone what he is really like?

The reason most people have difficulty describing someone is threefold: (1) they do not look at details; (2) they do not know what to look for; and (3) they do not have the vocabulary to depict what they do see.

Begin, then, by making a study of the person you want to describe.

First, his physical appearance. Consider height and breadth; consider particular features like the nose, eyes, mouth, and chin; consider his voice and his gestures.

Second, his personality make-up. Consider his disposition, his attitudes, his values, his virtues and vices.

Next, *look* at the "info sheet" on the next page. Think about the adjectives in each group. Notice that while the words in one group are often similar, they are not exact synonyms. There is a difference between obese and plump, between absent-minded and heedless, between fickle and vacillating. If you are uncertain about the meanings of some of these words, you may want to consult a dictionary to clarify distinctions.

Now, *use* the "info sheet." Check or circle words that are appropriate for the character you wish to describe. Remember that these are possibilities only; the choice of the right word is more important than the simple using of many words.

Finally, *rewrite* the description of your friend that you wrote at the beginning of this lesson. Better yet, forget it completely and start over. If you have really thought about your friend's appearance and personality, if you have chosen descriptive words carefully and with discrimination, the result should be a verbal portrait that is forceful, accurate, and meaningful.

- -

- -

- -

- -

- -

1. talkative, loquacious, garrulous, verbose
   taciturn, reticent, laconic

2. active, industrious, diligent, agile
   indolent, idle, sluggish, inert

3. obese, fat, plump, chubby
   thin, slim, slender, lithe

4. arrogant, lordly, imperious, domineering
   humble, gentle, docile, submissive

5. abstemious, frugal, moderate, temperate
   gluttonous, wanton, self-indulgent, intemper-
   ate

6. absent-minded, heedless
   alert, attentive

7. rational, reasonable, sagacious, shrewd
   irrational, senseless, foolish, obtuse

8. apprehensive, timid, cowardly
   confident, audacious, gallant, intrepid

9. amateur, dilettante
   professional, expert

10. amiable, good-natured, charming, pleasant
    churlish, morose, sullen, disagreeable

11. eager, ardent, intense, passionate
    apathetic, indifferent, stolid, phlegmatic

12. awkward, clumsy, boorish, gauche
    dexterous, adroit, clever

13. barbaric, merciless, brutal, uncouth
    civilized, humane, tender, urbane

14. beautiful, handsome, exquisite, elegant
    ugly, grotesque, hideous, repulsive

15. generous, altruistic, bountiful
    avaricious, niggardly, parsimonious

16. candid, sincere, naive, truthful
    crafty, cunning, subtle, deceitful

17. determined, resolute
    fickle, hesitant, vacillating

18. devoted, incorruptible, loyal, constant
    capricious, faithless, untrustworthy

19. healthy, vigorous
    frail, emaciated

20. large, immense, gigantic, broad, bulky
    diminutive, little, insignificant, microscopic,
    petty

15. MALAPROPISMS

A *malapropism* is a word misused—misused ridiculously or pompously. This misuse takes its name from Mrs. Malaprop, a character in *The Rivals*, a play by Richard Brinsley Sheridan; Mrs. Malaprop is notorious for her misapplication of words.

I. Working with malapropisms can be fun. Try to identify the malapropism in each of the sentences below; then suggest the word Mrs. Malaprop really wanted.

Example: "Come, Sir . . . lead the way and we'll precede."
Answer: precede—proceed (The malapropism is, of course, *precede*. If someone *leads*, we cannot *precede*, that is, go before. The word Mrs. Malaprop really wants is *proceed*.)

1. "The point we would request of you is that you will promise to forget this fellow—to illiterate him, I say, quite from your memory."

----

2. "There's a little intricate hussy for you!"

----

3. "I would by no means wish a daughter of mine to be a progeny of learning."

----

4. "She should have a supercilious knowledge in accounts."

----

5. "I hope you will represent her to the Captain as . . . not altogether illegible."

----

6. "Your being Sir Anthony's son, Captain, would itself be a sufficient accommodation."

----

7. "He is the very pine-apple of politeness!"

----

8. "She's as headstrong as an allegory on the banks of the Nile."

----

9. "I am sorry to say, Sir Anthony, that my affluence over my niece is very small."

----

10. "I laid my positive conjunction on her never to think on the fellow again."

II. Now try these more modern malapropisms.

1. The ingenuity of the young girl's appearance made everyone want to protect her.

----

2. I always knew he suffered from allusions of grandeur!

----

3. Many of the conquerors of the past have picturesque epitaphs; for example, Alexander *the Great*, Richard *the Lion-Hearted*, and Charles *the Good*.

----

4. After Tim swallowed the poison, we immediately gave him an anecdote, and he survived.

----

5. "Did you see the news story?" she cried. "He has a wife in New York, another in Los Angeles, and a third in Chicago! He's a polygon!"

----

6. The honeymooners were thoroughly enjoying their first days of martial life.

----

7. "She's a croquette!" cried seventeen-year-old Bill. "I just won't go steady with a girl who's a croquette!"

----

8. The beautiful young starlet went to Vietnam to boost the morals of the troops.

----

9. "He's such a fine philanderer," the dowager exclaimed. "He's donated millions of dollars to worthy causes."

----

10. "I'm really very ascetic," she said proudly. "I love operas and Renaissance art and lovely old books."

----

16. *TIME* Enough . . .

One of the most fascinating writing styles popular today is that used by the writers of *Time*, the weekly news magazine. An analysis of this style will increase your vocabulary, heighten your appreciation as a reader, and improve your own writing skill. Just follow Steps I, II, III, and IV.

Step I. First read the story below. It was published in the July 6, 1970 issue of *Time* (page 8). Read it at your ordinary reading rate.

Who Owns the Stars and Stripes?

In a vanished time of simpler Fourths of July, Woodrow Wilson proudly hailed the American flag as "the emblem of our unity." For many Americans on Independence Day 1970, to unfurl, or not unfurl, the front-porch flag is an unsettling dilemma. What was once an easy, automatic rite of patriotism has become in many cases a considered political act, burdened with overtones and conflicting meanings greater than Old Glory was ever meant to bear. In the tug of war for the nation's will and soul, the flag has somehow become the symbolic rope. It takes no Swiftian eye to be astonished by what Americans are doing with—and to—the national banner.

Some, mostly the defiant young, blow their noses on it, sleep in it, set it afire, or wear it to patch the seat of their trousers. In response, others wave it with defensive pride, crack skulls in its name, and fly it from their garbage trucks, police cars and skyscraper scaffolds. In pride or put-on, Pop or protest, Old Glory's heraldry blazons battered campers and Indianapolis 500 racers, silver pins and trash bins, glittering cowboy vests and ample bikinied chests. The flag has become the emblem of America's disunity, and, in a land where once only wars abroad set it fluttering in vast numbers, the caricature of a new conflict is raging right at home. The old meaning still persists; hardly any American could escape a thrill of pride when Neil Armstrong planted his vertebrate flag on the airless moon. But some Americans could also sympathize with the emotion that moved a student at Kent State to rip down a flag after the shootings. It is as if two cultures, both of them oddly brandishing the same banner, were arrayed in some 18th century battle painting, the young whirling in defiant rock carmagnole against the panoplied Silent Majority.

*   *   *

"Within the kids' lifetimes, this flag hasn't stood for the things it stood for when John Glenn and I were young," says Allen Brown, a Cincinnati lawyer. "The flag then was still the flag of the dream. It's hard for us to understand kids who have only a book idea of the flag. They didn't see men die within the framework of that idealism of World War II. It's as if people see the flag the way Moses saw the golden calf. Half our population remembers it as a blessing, and the other half, who have grown up since World War II, see it only as a golden calf. If only both could get beyond the symbolism."

Step II. Now reread the story. This time read slowly. Force yourself to be conscious of individual words and word order. Forget the *what* (subject matter) of the story; concentrate on the *how* (the writing style).

Step III. Proceed to an analysis of *Time*'s style.

1. Note use of interesting or unusual words. "Panoplied" is an odd word to appear in a news magazine; so is "carmagnole" (a dance and song popular during the French Revolution).

   List below *five* more words, unusual in themselves or unusual in context.

   ----------------------------   ----------------------------

   ----------------------------   ----------------------------

   ----

2. Note use of apt phrases. We generally think of a "flag" as flying free, and to most of us the word "vertebrate" suggests rigidity. Yet in this story the words are combined to form the phrase "vertebrate flag." It has a paradoxical flavor, hasn't it? (The paradox, by the way, is an *apparent* contradiction and is a favorite technique with *Time* writers.)

   List below three more apt phrases.

   ----

3. Note use of vivid verbs. Isn't "heraldry blazons battered campers" more effective than the milder "heraldry decorates battered campers"?

   Can you find three more vivid verbs?

   ----

4. Note the skillful use of parallel structure. In the second paragraph, for example, the writer says that some

   "blow their noses on it,
     sleep in it,
     set it afire,
     or wear it . . ."

   List below another example of parallel structure.

   ----

5. Alliteration (the repetition of the initial sound in two or more words) is another favorite device. One good example is "skyscraper scaffolds."

   Can you find three more examples of alliteration?

   ----

6. Note the use of contrast. The writer mentions in the same sentence "battered campers" and "Indianapolis 500 racers," thus sharpening both images.

List two more examples of contrast.

----

7. Many writers *imply* at least as much as they *state*. Thus, in paragraph one, "to unfurl, or not unfurl" echoes Hamlet's "To be or not to be"—emphasizing the general feeling of indecision.
   a. What is implied by the repeated use of the phrase "Old Glory"?

   ----

   b. What is implied by the phrase "defiant rock carmagnole" at the end of paragraph two?

   ----

   c. What does the adjective "panoplied" suggest about the Silent Majority?

   ----

   d. Note the ambiguity (open to several interpretations) of the title, "Who Owns the Stars and Stripes?" What interpretation is logical if the word *Who* is emphasized?

   ----

   e. What interpretation is logical if the word *Owns* is emphasized?

Step IV. You should be ready now to tackle *Time*! Below are *three* related facts drawn from another *Time* story. Using as many of *Time*'s stylistic techniques as possible, write a paragraph based on these facts.

   1. Richard Nixon knows people enjoy visiting the White House.
   2. During his first year in office he was host to 50,000 guests.
   3. Various types of entertainment were provided for the guests.

Is the finished product *Time*-ly?

17. TRAVEL WITH A THESAURUS

An invaluable tool for any speaker or writer is a thumb-worn copy of Roget's *Thesaurus*. With it your writing can become forceful—vigorous—robust—virile—dynamic—potent—powerful—spirited—incisive—lively. With it your writing can become precise. But first you must learn to use it easily and well.

Step I. Let's begin with the verb WALK, certainly a word we use often. Look it up in the Index at the back of the *Thesaurus*. You will find more than a dozen entries under WALK. Choose the one that seems closest to the meaning you intend—probably *move*. Note the page number and turn to the proper section. Here you will find synonyms divided into verbs, nouns, adjectives, adverbs, etc. You are now ready to go to work.

Each of the sentences below demands a specific near-synonym of WALK. Consider the subject matter and tone of each sentence and try to determine the exact word that has been omitted. To assist you, we have given you the first letter of each missing word.

1. The hungry mountain lion p_____ through the woods, looking for a deer or an antelope.

2. Weary from his long day's labor, the miner p_____ slowly home.

3. Swinging his ivory-headed cane, the elegant gentleman s_____ down the street.

4. The Greek soldiers m_____ twenty miles down the road to the sea.

5. The young father, waiting for the arrival of his first child, p_____ back and forth in the waiting room of the hospital.

6. It was a hot and lazy day, and he had nothing to do. So he decided to a_____ over to his friend's house for a little reminiscing.

7. With a new dress, new pumps, new everything, the new Miss America decided to p_____ along the boardwalk.

8. The one-year-old t_____ uncertainly from one chair to another.

9. With nowhere to go and nothing to do, the salesman w_____ about the strange town for two hours.

10. The five-year-old, proudly wearing his first pair of long pants, s_____ before his friends.

Step II. This exercise is similar to the first—but here you are *not* given the first letter of the missing word. The original word, this time, is LAMENT. Check it in the Index; then turn to the correct section. (Remember to consult more than one section if it seems necessary.) Do *not* use the same near-synonym more than once.

1. Terrified and tearful, the child _____ for his mother.

2. As his master approached with a folded newspaper, the mischievous terrier _____.

3. The lover _____ as he watched his lovely fiancée close the door.

4. Finding the pain almost intolerable, the patient _____.

5. Furious at himself and at his teacher, the boy _____ darkly.

6. As he wrote a check for his income tax, the irate citizen _____ mightily.

7. Hysterical, with shoulders shaking, the girl _____ as the firemen led her out of the burning house.

8. After the telegram arrived, she _____ softly, but her _____ continued for hours. (two forms of the same word)

9. Beyond control, beyond restraint, the women _____ loudly as their husbands were carried from the collapsed mine shaft.

10. Without sound, they _____ their dead—but the bent bodies and the leaden eyes spoke eloquently of their sorrow.

Step III. Here is a monologue. With the help of a *Thesaurus*, replace the over-tired "get's" or "got's" with different, more precise words. At times it may be necessary to change a few words or the word order; do not use a particular replacement more than once.

"I want to *get* (1)_____ a book from the library," Mary said to Jean, "but first let's *get* (2)_____ our books from the lockers. And I've *got* to (3)_____ hurry because I've *got* (4)_____ to *get* (5)_____ home before four o'clock! My mother wants to *get* (6)_____ a new hat, but before she can go downtown, she'll have to *get* (7)_____ a taxi. If she doesn't *get* (8)_____ a new hat, my father will *get* (9)_____ angry.

Perhaps they'll *get* (10)_____ to know your parents at the dance, Jean. I'd like it if they *got* (11)_____ to become friends. After all, they've *got* (12)_____ a lot in common.

By the way, Jean, I *got* (13)_____ an "A" in history; I think I can *get* (14)_____ my mother to let me *get* (15)_____ new shoes! I could have *gotten* (16)_____ an "A" in algebra, too, but I just don't *get* (17)_____ those equations. If it weren't for math, I could *get* (18)_____ on the honor roll this month.

Let's *get* (19)_____ going, Jean. I want to see if I *got* (20)_____ a letter from my boyfriend!"

Now you are ready to use the *Thesaurus* as it was meant to be used—to improve your writing. It will, as was promised, make your writing more precise, more concise, and more interesting. Adopt it as a traveling companion, and use it whenever you are in doubt about your diction or whenever you find yourself indulging in needless repetition.

18. CORRELATED COUPLETS

Rhyming couplets are a delight to the ear and a challenge to the wits. Why not master versification and vocabulary simultaneously, coupling them through couplet construction?

I. Here's an Ogden Nash couplet:

> Here's a good rule of thumb:
> Too clever is dumb.

First enjoy it. On what kind of occasion is it "dumb" to be too clever? Then note the rhyme scheme—"thumb" rhyming with "dumb." Next analyze the meter:

> Here's a good / rule of thumb:
> Too clev / er is dumb.

You may recognize it as anapestic dimeter with one variation. Dimeter, remember, means two feet to a line—in this case, two anapestic feet. And an anapestic foot is made up of three syllables: two unaccented (˘˘) and the third accented (—). (To get the anapestic rhythm, strike your pencil against a book three times, twice softly, once hard; then repeat. Each group of three strikes is an anapestic foot. Two feet = dimeter.)

Now try out your new skill. Here's an anapestic dimeter line that will serve as the first line of a couplet:

> If you try / to be free

Make up a second line (also of anapestic dimeter) that rhymes with *free* and that makes *sense*—or nonsense! Ready? Here are a couple of possible second lines:

> I will chain / you to me.
>
> *or*
>
> The whole world / you must flee.

- -

Does yours rhyme? Does the meter match? Try one more—but this time *you* write the complete couplet:

- -

- -

II. Now return to the original Ogden Nash couplet. What would be a good title for this couplet? Write down some suggestions:

- -

- -

- -

Ogden Nash's title is "Reflection on Ingenuity." Is it more effective than yours? (It should be!) Why? Notice how the touch of pomposity in the title sharpens the simple couplet.

III. This time we'll invert the procedure used in II above. Here's a title; *you* provide a suitable couplet! (Consult a dictionary if necessary.)

"Sobriquet for a Sober Sojourner"

"The Lamentable Story of Gerrymandering"

"An Inferno of Despicable Despots"

"The Infallible Felicity of Feminine Logic"

Couplet construction can be a life-saver in many situations—to break the ice at a party, to pass the time while waiting for the dentist, to numb your brain into sleep. And it will make you rhyme-conscious, meter-conscious, and word-conscious! What more can you ask?

19. UNDER A MICROSCOPE

Place these paragraphs under a microscope—well, figuratively, anyway! Study this short piece of writing as a scientist studies a biological specimen. They are the first four paragraphs of O. Henry's short story "The Cop and the Anthem."

On his bench in Madison Square, Soapy moved uneasily. When wild geese honk high of nights, and when women without sealskin coats grow kind to their husbands, and when Soapy moves uneasily on his bench in the park, you may know that winter is near at hand.

A dead leaf fell in Soapy's lap. That was Jack Frost's card. Jack is kind to the regular denizens of Madison Square and gives fair warning of his annual call. At the corners of four streets, he hands his pasteboards to the North Wind, footman of the mansion of All Outdoors, so that the inhabitants thereof may make ready.

Soapy's mind became cognizant of the fact that the time had come for him to resolve himself into a singular Committee of Ways and Means to provide against the coming rigor. And therefore he moved uneasily on his bench.

The hibernatorial ambitions of Soapy were not of the highest. In them there were no considerations of Mediterranean cruises, of soporific Southern skies, or drifting in the Vesuvian Bay. Three months on the Island was what his soul craved. Three months of assured board and bed and congenial company, safe from Boreas and the blue-coats, seemed to Soapy the essence of things desirable.

Procedure:

1. Read the selection several times—carefully.

2. Underline any words that are unfamiliar. Write them on the lines below. Next to each write the dictionary definition.

----

3. Circle figurative phrases like "Jack Frost's card."

4. Bracket examples of parallel structure; for instance, [When wild geese . . .] [when women . . .] [when Soapy moves . . .].

5. Deliberate repetition of several phrases can be an effective writing device. Can you find a group of words in paragraph #1 that are *almost* exactly repeated in paragraph #3?

----

6. Contrast is another good writing device. In this selection there is general contrast between the *low-level* subject matter (the story of a deadbeat, a tramp) and the *high-level* allusions and vocabulary.

    a. In paragraph #3 there is a contrast concerning Soapy. Can you find it?

    ----

    b. In paragraph #4 there is a contrast concerning places. Can you find it?

    ----

7. Now read the selection again. You *should* enjoy it more this time.

8. Some additional questions for you:

    a. *Why* did O. Henry use such "elevated" language when he was writing about a vagrant?

    ----

    b. *Why* did O. Henry use allusions to Jack Frost, to Vesuvian Bay, to Mediterranean cruises?

    ----

    c. Is the selection successful for you? ------

    Are you interested in reading the rest of the story? ------

    By now you may like or dislike the results of O. Henry's art, but you should have a clearer idea of what art is, in writing. The next time *you* write, consider using some of O. Henry's techniques: the unexpected word, the colorful allusion, parallel structure, repetition, or the sharp contrast. All are helpful; all will strengthen your skill with words and your ability to express yourself effectively.

20. WORD BOOKS

One way to sharpen your awareness of words is to acquire the habit of browsing through a few of the many word books available. They are reservoirs of fascinating information: stories about words, international parallels, origins of intriguing phrases, insights into our national heritage.

To help you get interested in some of these word books, we have listed a few questions for three of them. By the time you have found the answers, you will be "hooked"—and will find yourself turning to the books at odd moments.

I. *A Dictionary of Contemporary American Usage*, by Bergen Evans and Cornelia Evans, Random House, New York, 1957

  1. Would you rather be called a gourmet, a gourmand, or a glutton? Why?

  2. What is crossword-puzzle English?

  3. What does *davenport* mean to an American? To an Englishman?

  4. How does popular meaning differ from Emerson's meaning for his phrase "hitch your wagon to a star"?

  5. Why are people interested in an international language? Name *three* suggested international languages.

  6. What is an artist? An artiste? An artisan?

7. Give an example of a mixed metaphor.

----

8. What is the difference between a nickname and a sobriquet?

----

9. What are the *three* possible plural forms of *rhinoceros*?

----

10. What is journalese?

II. *The American Language*, by H. L. Mencken (Fourth Edition), Alfred A. Knopf, New York, 1962

1. List *eight* given names popular in Tennessee.

----

2. What are the English terms that correspond to the following American terms: *public school, class, principal, commencement*?

----

3. What is the probable origin of the verb *lynch*?

----

4. List *three* word relations of *motorcade*.

----

5. What is a "lucky-dip"?

----

6. What is the possible meaning of *ish ke bibble*?

----

7. List *ten* unusual words ending in *-fest*.

----

8. How did "vamoose" come to have its present meaning?

----

9. List *five* words or phrases coined by Walter Winchell.

----

10. List *five* unusual place-names in West Virginia.

III. *Funk and Wagnalls Standard Handbook of Synonyms, Antonyms, and Prepositions*, by James C. Fernald, Funk and Wagnalls, New York, 1947

1. What is the difference between *flare* and *flash*? Between *glare* and *glow*?

----

2. List *ten* synonyms for *embarrass*.

----

3. List *five* antonyms for *barbarous*.

----

4. The verb *encourage* can be used with five different prepositions. List the *five* prepositions and indicate correct usage in each case.

----

5. What is the difference between a *theory* and a *hypothesis*?

----

6. If you find *lazy* insufficient in describing someone, what other three synonyms could you use?

----

7. What is the difference between an *archetype* and a *prototype*.

----

8. "*Annals*, *archives*, *chronicles*, *biographies*, and *records* furnish the materials of *history*." Explain the meaning of each italicized word.

----

9. Why would we prefer to call our soldiers *formidable* rather than *dangerous*?

----

10. If I wish to say that I overcame my enemy, I can say I --------------------- him or

--------------------- him.

Other Word Books:

Brewer: *Dictionary of Phrase and Fable*
Crabb: *English Synonyms Explained*
Rodall: *The Word Finder*
Morris: *Dictionary of Word and Phrase Origins*

Part IV. *Word Wizardry*

Each of the twenty lessons in this section presents a group of related words spiced with a soupçon of nonsense. Each is designed to heighten your awareness of words and, through this new awareness, to extend and enrich your knowledge.

One lesson, for example, will remind you that a group of letters may form one word when read from left to right, and quite another word when read from right to left. Working on this lesson, "Forward—Reverse," should be fun; it should also strengthen your realization that words are symbols—that they mean only what we humans want them to mean. Another, "Car Caravan," will help you to understand automobile manufacturers and the clever way they manipulate words to appeal to consumers. Still another, "A Rocket to the Moon," brings together many words related to space travel that you already know, a few common words that now have additional meanings, and a few you may not know at all. You will be surprised to realize that a field as new as space travel already has its own vocabulary—and the twenty words in this lesson are only the less technical!

Each of these lessons will take only a few minutes of your time. Each, too, will jog your memory and sharpen your word manipulation skills. Above all, each is a challenge—a challenge to a word duel! Dare you accept?

1. COLOR COMBINATIONS

In the blank or blanks, fill in the word or words that satisfy the definition. Each answer contains the name of a color.

Example: an infant with congenital cyanosis
Answer: blue baby

------------- ------------- 1. a member of a noble or socially prominent family

---------------------------- 2. a British soldier

------------- ------------- 3. jealous

------------- ------------- 4. an American type of Roquefort

---------------------------- 5. a scoundrel

---------------------------- 6. an inexperienced person

------------- ------------- 7. a peace offering

---------------------------- 8. Kentucky lawn

------------- ------------- 9. a large bee

------------- ------------- 10. a "go-ahead" signal

---------------------------- 11. a robin

------------- ------------- 12. the flower for brides

------------- ------------- 13. puritanical American laws

---------------------------- 14. a part of every classroom

------------- ------------- 15. a baked pudding containing apples

---------------------------- 16. a railroad station porter

------------- ------------- 17. to edit

------------- ------------- 18. a harmless fib

---------------------------- 19. a U.S. legal-tender note

---------------------------- 20. a detailed plan, especially of a building

---------------------------- 21. a payment extorted by intimidation

------------- ------------- 22. a kind of malaria

---------------------------- 23. the crest of a wave

---------------------------- 24. a woman having literary tastes

---------------------------- 25. a glass building for growing plants

2. NAMESAKES

Famous people have famous namesakes. Using the clues given below, see how many of the "namesakes" you can identify.

Example: a perennial hay grass named after an American naturalist
Answer: timothy

--------------- --------------- 1. very thin bread toasted till crisp, named after a famous soprano

------------------------------- 2. a breakfast favorite named after the Roman goddess of grain

--------------- --------------- 3. patties of ground beef named after an English physician

------------------------------- 4. a lunch-time favorite named after an earl who was a gambler who hated to interrupt the game

------------------------------- 5. a candy, popular in the South, made of brown sugar and pecans, named after a French count

------------- ------------- 6. a beef cooked in consommé and sour cream, named after a Russian diplomat

------------------------------- 7. a three-layered French pastry filled with custard or cream, with the same name as a nineteenth-century emperor and general

------------------------------- 8. a plaid, or knitted socks, patterned after a clan tartan

------------------------------- 9. a collarless sweater that buttons in the front, named after a British earl

------------------------------- 10. a tailored overcoat or an overstuffed couch named after a gentlemanly earl

------------------------------- 11. a low-crowned soft hat for men, named after a character in a play

------------------------------- 12. a waterproof raincoat named after a Scottish chemist

------------------------------- 13. a woolen cap with a wide, flat, circular crown named after the hero of a poem by Robert Burns

------------------------------- 14. an annual entertainment award named after a wealthy Texan

------------------------------- 15. an overstuffed footstool named after a Turkish ruler

--------------- --------------- 16. a favorite crib toy named after a U.S. President who liked big-game hunting

------------------------------- 17. a blacktop road based on layers of crushed stone, named after a Scot

------------------------------- 18. a book of maps named after the Greek demigod who reportedly held up the world

------------------------------- 19. an animal (or human) who stays apart from the herd, named after a San Antonio cattleman

------------------------------- 20. a beheading device named after a French physician

3. A METHOD IN MANIA

Here is a word game that you will enjoy. Simply follow the directions and you will find that you know some words you didn't know you knew!

I. Mania. This is a root coming from the Greek word meaning "madness"; hence, it means having a great enthusiasm for something, a craze for something. Keep this in mind as you try to match up the two columns below. If you have trouble with some of the words, look at the clues listed below the columns. They should help you to make "educated" guesses!

```
_ _ _ _   1. dipsomania      a. a persistent abnormal impulse to steal
_ _ _ _   2. pyromania       b. delusions of grandeur
_ _ _ _   3. kleptomania     c. an excessive fondness for what is English
_ _ _ _   4. monomania       d. an irresistible impulse to start fires
_ _ _ _   5. megalomania     e. a need to tell lies
_ _ _ _   6. egomania        f. a fascination with numbers
_ _ _ _   7. bibliomania     g. morbid self-esteem
_ _ _ _   8. arithmomania    h. an uncontrollable craving for alcoholic drink
_ _ _ _   9. mythomania      i. an enthusiasm for collecting books
_ _ _ _  10. Anglomania      j. an obsession on one topic
```

Clues

pyro—Think of *pyro*technics, *pyre*.
mono—Remember *mono*theism, *mono*tone, *mono*tony.
mega—Recall *mega*phone, *mega*cycle.
ego—You already know *ego*tism.
biblio—Remember *biblio*graphy, *biblio*phile.
arithm—Of course you know *arithm*etic!
myth—You're familiar with *myth*ical and *myth*ology.
Anglo—There's *Anglo*-Saxon and there's *Anglo*-American.

II. Cide. This is a root that means "act of killing." Keep this in mind as you try to match up the two columns below, the "crime" column with the "victim" column. If you have trouble with some of the words, check the clues listed below the columns. They should help you.

	CRIME		VICTIM
_ _ _ _	1. homicide	*a.*	mother
_ _ _ _	2. suicide	*b.*	brother
_ _ _ _	3. matricide	*c.*	king
_ _ _ _	4. patricide	*d.*	race
_ _ _ _	5. regicide	*e.*	wife
_ _ _ _	6. fratricide	*f.*	human being
_ _ _ _	7. infanticide	*g.*	sister
_ _ _ _	8. genocide	*h.*	father
_ _ _ _	9. sororicide	*i.*	self
_ _ _ _	10. uxoricide	*j.*	child

Clues

matri—Remember *mater*nal, *mater*nity.
patri—And *pater*nal and *pater*nity.
fratri—There's *frater*nal order or a *frater*nity.
soror—Or a *soror*ity.
infanti—Obvious in *infant* and *infanti*le.
regi—You know *reg*al, of course.
homo—And everyone knows *Homo sapiens*.
gen—Familiar in *gen*der, *gen*us, *gen*ealogy.

4. HUNTING HOMONYMS

I. *Homonyms* are words that sound alike but are different in spelling and in meaning. With a little astute guessing, you should be able to discover the correct pair of homonyms for each of the following sentences.

Example: For lunch the child _____ a bowl of soup and _____ crackers.
Answer: ate *and* eight

1. She was too exhausted and _____ to survive another _____ of agony.

2. She let the annoying boy have another _____ of cake in order to keep _____ at the dinner table.

3. After taking a bath, wash off the _____ on the tub; then _____ out the wash-cloth.

4. The cowboy mounted his horse and nonchalantly _____ down the main _____ of the frontier town.

5. I plan to _____ to Europe on that ocean liner after completing the _____ of my house.

6. He had just enough money to cover his bus _____ and admission to the county _____.

7. In the days of King Arthur, a _____ fought during the day but returned to the castle at _____.

8. The policeman mounted on the white _____ shouted at the demonstrator in a _____ voice.

9. You are expected to sit with your sister at the birthday luncheon; don't _____ her until all the guests have finished their _____.

10. He decorated his horse's _____, since he was to ride in procession with the _____ party.

11. The Air _____, some people think, is the _____ of the modern army.

12. His _____ quickened as he approached the _____ of the Wendell Estate.

13. If you work hard enough on this _____, you will _____ your chance of failure.

14. The mule carried the _____ of equipment to the site of the newly found _____ of gold.

15. A _____ of people, all planning to _____ canned food during the truck strike, were emptying the shelves of the supermarket.

16. The king sighed as he looked out the window at the wet fields; it seemed to _____ constantly during his dismal _____.

101 Ways to Learn Vocabulary

17. The English _____ stepped off the gangplank onto the _____ after a stormy Atlantic crossing.

18. You will understand the _____ issues behind the strike after you watch the next _____ of film.

19. "_____ your face so that it will be warmed by the _____ of the sun," she suggested.

20. During the days that the tiger terrorized that hamlet, the villagers would often _____ at night that they would not be the animal's next _____.

II. After you have completed "Hunting Homonyms," you may enjoy creating a few sentences of your own. Use the pairs of homonyms listed below. Construct each sentence so that there is at least one clue to the correct answer.

1. AIR and HEIR

----

2. WHOLE and HOLE

----

3. BRAKE and BREAK

----

4. HEARD and HERD

----

5. SEEN and SCENE

----

6. SUITE and SWEET

----

7. PLAIN and PLANE

----

8. WASTE and WAIST

----

9. FEAT and FEET

----

10. KNEAD and NEED

----

5. ALL SHAPES AND SIZES

In these days of ready-to-wear, everything comes in assorted shapes and sizes—even words! In the first exercise, you are invited to play with sizes; in the second, with shapes.

I. Sizes

To satisfy each definition below, find a word that incorporates *short, tall, low,* or *high.* (The blanks indicate whether the answer is one word, two words, or hyphenated.)

Example: a drink of diluted spirits
Answer: *high*ball

1. _____   1. an intellectual
2. _____ - _____   2. dejected; depressed
3. _____ - _____   3. not lasting long
4. _____   4. overbearing in the use of power
5. _____   _____   5. a fantastic tale (colloquial)
6. _____   _____   6. farce; burlesque; slapstick
7. _____   _____   7. open sections of the ocean
8. _____   8. a deficiency; a defect
9. _____   9. a rapid method of writing
10. _____   10. a main road
11. _____   11. a crisp, unsweetened biscuit
12. _____   12. low or level country
13. _____   13. a chest of drawers on a tablelike base
14. _____   14. to give less than the correct amount of change to
15. _____ - _____   15. contemptible; base

II. Shapes

To satisfy each definition below, find a word that incorporates *round* or *square.*

1. _____   1. the act of gathering together cattle on the range
2. _____   _____   2. an honest person; one who plays fairly
3. _____   _____   3. a dance for four couples
4. _____   4. a simple song with refrain
5. _____   5. a cabin on the quarterdeck of a ship
6. _____   _____   6. length times width

7. _____ ____ _____   7. a cut of the thigh of a steer

8. _____ _____   8. a written petition with signatures in a circle

9. _____ _____   9. fair or honest treatment

10. _____   10. circuitous; indirect

6. CAR CARAVAN

In this age of the "hard sell," automobile manufacturers are no longer content to settle for simple trade names. Each sports car, each compact, must have its own identifying tag—and the wilder, the better! We have taken fifteen cars and have dreamed up descriptions suggested by their names. How many can you identify? If you must, you can look through the list of names at the bottom of the page.

Example: This car has the speed and stamina of a battle horse. It also is suitable for a Prince Charming.
Answer: Charger (Dodge)

_____ 1. This car is a celestial vehicle that streaks through outer space.

_____ 2. This car is as swift and graceful as a South African deer.

_____ 3. This car is ferocious and powerful and is named after a spotted feline.

_____ 4. This car almost sings in flight! Its owner should always be ready for a carefree frolic.

_____ 5. This car is only half-tamed. It will be preferred by twentieth-century cowboys and rangers.

_____ 6. This car is as formidable and flashing as a pirate's sword; it has "derring-do"!

_____ 7. This car is perfect for the wealthy sophisticate who vacations on the Mediterranean coast and revels in glamour!

_____ 8. This car should appeal to lovers of Indian lore. It is even capable of producing thunder, lightning, and rain.

_____ 9. This car is exactly right for big-game hunters; it promises danger, excitement, and romance!

_____ 10. This car is elfin-like. It is perfect for the mischievous joker.

_____ 11. This car has the sinewy, hidden power of a mountain lion or panther.

_____ 12. This car is for the brave. Its owner should have a stout heart, even when outnumbered.

_____ 13. This car is astronomical! It suggests splendid assemblages and brilliant gatherings.

_____ 14. This car has the untamed fury and violence of a North American feline. A man engaged in a reckless business enterprise may use it.

_____ 15. This car has dignity and savoir-faire. It is suitable for the European traveler or for the U.S.A. tourer.

Wildcat	Cutlass	Skylark
Mustang	Comet	Riviera
Thunderbird	Galaxie	Cougar
Continental	Jaguar	Sprite
Impala	Valiant	Safari

7. NUMBER SENSE

Divide *octa*gon by *bi*sect and you get *quad*ruplets—well, almost! But most "number" words do have a prefix that acts as a "built-in" clue. Take a quick look at the clues below; then see how many of the number words you can guess.

Clues

mono = one	*tri* = three	*quint* = five
uni = one	*quad* (*quart*) = four	*octa* = eight
bi = two	*penta* = five	*deca* = ten

-------------------------- 1. a group of four

-------------------------- 2. a three-wheeled vehicle moved by pedals

-------------------------- 3. a fourth of a gallon

-------------------------- 4. to cut into two

-------------------------- 5. three plays or three novels

-------------------------- 6. five sisters and/or brothers born at one time

-------------------------- 7. a five-sided figure

-------------------------- 8. speaking two languages

-------------------------- 9. one of three identical copies

-------------------------- 10. one-sided, as a decision

-------------------------- 11. a four-legged animal

-------------------------- 12. an eyeglass for one eye

-------------------------- 13. to kill one out of ten

-------------------------- 14. an eight-footed fish

-------------------------- 15. exclusive (or single) control of a product or industry

-------------------------- 16. occurring every two years

-------------------------- 17. a group of three

-------------------------- 18. a ten-year period

-------------------------- 19. two-headed muscles

-------------------------- 20. a speech uttered by one person

8. NUMBER NONSENSE

Combine a number with one or more other words to form a phrase that satisfies the definition at the right. (You may use various forms of numbers—e.g., one or first, two or second.)

Example: Ali Baba's opposition
Answer: forty thieves

----------------------------- 1. used; not new

----------------------------- 2. absolutely top quality

----------------------------- 3. one who bluffs, especially in poker

----------------------------- 4. a person who is unneeded or in the way

----------------------------- 5. a girl's favorite birthday

----------------------------- 6. a summer holiday

----------------------------- 7. what a cat has

----------------------------- 8. newspapermen

----------------------------- 9. the assistant to the captain

----------------------------- 10. sympathizers or supporters of an enemy

----------------------------- 11. an intensive interrogation

----------------------------- 12. advanced age with enfeebled mentality and childishness

----------------------------- 13. the Colossus at Rhodes and other marvels

----------------------------- 14. Lincoln's way of saying eighty

----------------------------- 15. an ideal group for golfing

----------------------------- 16. a store specializing in inexpensive items

----------------------------- 17. emergency help

----------------------------- 18. the social elite of years ago

----------------------------- 19. something that causes a short-lived sensation

----------------------------- 20. deceitful; hypocritical

9. TALKING TYPES

We seldom talk, or even speak. We cry, shout, ask, assert, and whisper. In fact, people utter noises in so many ways we have dozens of words to describe this action. How many types of speaking can you identify?

The first letter of each answer is given. The number of blanks corresponds to the number of letters missing.

r _ _ _ _   1. to talk in a wild or vehement manner

s _ _ _ _ _ _ _   2. to speak with involuntary pauses

m _ _ _ _ _ _   3. to utter in a low tone and a complaining manner

b _ _ _ _ _ _   4. to speak foolishly or thoughtlessly

g _ _ _ _ _ _   5. to talk unintelligibly

d _ _ _ _ _   6. to speak in a dull, monotonous voice

m _ _ _ _ _ _   7. to speak with a soft, continuous sound

e _ _ _ _ _ _ _ _ _ _   8. to utter suddenly and briefly

h _ _ _ _ _ _ _ _ _   9. to speak noisily and vehemently

c _ _ _ _ _ _   10. to chatter with shrill, broken sounds

b _ _ _ _ _   11. to utter inadvertently; to divulge (usually used with "out")

t _ _ _ _ _   12. to speak with a nasal tone

d _ _ _ _ _ _ _   13. to speak for oratorical effect

w _ _ _ _ _ _ _   14. to utter in low, plaintive sounds

c _ _ _ _   15. to talk in a familiar or informal manner

d _ _ _ _ _   16. to speak in a slow, lingering way

r _ _ _ _ _ _   17. to speak from memory

c _ _ _ _ _   18. to speak with a dismal, hollow voice

f _ _ _ _ _ _   19. to speak hesitatingly or brokenly

b _ _ _ _ _ _   20. to speak in sorrow or grief

10. OCCUPATIONAL HAZARD

The five men described below are in a state of total confusion. They have mixed up the materials with which (or on which) they work, and the adjective that is often used to describe their type of work. They have even lost the friend (in the same field of work) with whom they like to confer. Can you bring order out of chaos by returning the proper materials, adjective, and friend to each man? (Note that in each case when the words are correctly rearranged, an intelligible sentence results.)

1. The **haberdasher** looked at the *subpoena*, *capsules*, and *caucus* on the counter, then called to the *chemist* for *forensic* advice.

----

2. The **barrister,** who had great *restorative* ability, conferred with the *lobbyist* about the *grammar* and *poultices* necessary for the planned *cummerbund*.

----

3. The **academician** and his friend, the *tailor*, had *parliamentary* discussions about *indictment*, *statute*, and *plus fours*.

----

4. The **pharmacist** asked the *etymologist* about the *sartorial* powers of *quorum*, *semantics*, and *litigation*.

----

5. The **legislator,** bound by *erudite* law, argued with the *advocate* about the legality of the *sedatives* and *linguistics* and the validity of the *cravat*.

----

11. CONCLUSION CONFUSION

I. Each of the following phrases defines a word that ends in "-USION." How many can you identify?

> *Example:* the final part
> *Answer:* *conclu*sion

————usion	1. a false belief or opinion
—usion	2. the state of becoming united or blended
—————usion	3. a secret understanding between two or more people for fraudulent purposes
—————usion	4. an abundant quantity
—————usion	5. a state of retirement or solitude
————usion	6. a reference to someone or something, especially in the past
———usion	7. a false mental image or conception
———————usion	8. the transference of blood from one person to another
—————usion	9. the state of being kept out
—————usion	10. a bruise; an injury caused by a blunt instrument
—————usion	11. an uninvited, unwanted entry
——————usion	12. to disenchant; to disappoint
—————usion	13. the state of being accepted, "counted in"
—————usion	14. the act of spreading or disseminating
—————usion	15. in dentistry, the bringing together of the upper and lower teeth in proper alignment

II. Each of the following phrases defines a word that ends in "-ONIC." How many of these can you identify?

————onic	1. inveterate; continuing a long time
————onic	2. a kind of plague
———————onic	3. having many sounds or voices
—onic	4. something that invigorates or strengthens
—————onic	5. purely spiritual love
———onic	6. characterized by the difference between what is said and what is intended
—onic	7. pertaining to sound
—————onic	8. characterized by a violent whirling motion
—————onic	9. sarcastic; sneering

101 Ways to Learn Vocabulary

—————onic   10. theatrical; affected

——onic   11. pertaining to speech sounds

———onic   12. inspired as if by an evil spirit

—————onic   13. pertaining to a harmony of sounds

———onic   14. using few words; concise

———————onic   15. of or relating to a lover of music

12. SPORT STEW

Last week a Shakespearean scholar wrote the sports news for the local newspaper. Some of the terms were a little strange to him, and certainly his story seemed a little strange to his readers! Can you unscramble the story by taking the italicized words and placing them in the correct columns following the story? You should be able to bat 1000!

The golfer ran onto the *gridiron* and *dribbled* the *horsehide* down the *fairway*. A minute later his partner, a *cager*, grabbed a *racket*, dashed within *shooting distance* of the target, and hurled a *knuckle ball*. Their opponents went into a *huddle*, selected a *niblick*, donned *shin guards*, and cried "*Love!*" "*Tee off*," shouted the *touchback*; "another *pop fly* and it will be our chance to *serve!*" The cager grimaced; he tucked the *pigskin* under his arm, eluded the *hazard*, then *smashed* the ball over the net. The *24-second clock* indicated that the *inning* was almost over. The opposing team formed a *flying wedge*, decided on a *sacrifice hit*, and sent the *mashie* high against the *backboard*.

Meanwhile, on the nearby *diamond*, a *doubles* was being played. The *kick-off* was converted to a gross *putt* as the *volley* picked up speed, rounded the *pitcher's box*, sidestepped the *blitz*, and headed for the *hoop*. But, alas—the *catcher* *fumbled* the ball, tried a *forehand drive* for a *free throw*, and landed on the *green*. "Put in the *caddie!*" cried the *red dog*. "*Bunt* to the *time line!*" shouted another. Triumphantly the *fielder straight-armed* his way through the *scrimmage line* and sank a *hole in one!* It only remained for the *putter* to *punt* a short *homer*— and the *set* was over.

BASEBALL (12 terms)	FOOTBALL (12 terms)	GOLF (10 terms)
-------------------	-------------------	-------------------
-------------------	-------------------	-------------------
-------------------	-------------------	-------------------
-------------------	-------------------	-------------------
-------------------	-------------------	-------------------
-------------------	-------------------	-------------------
-------------------	-------------------	-------------------
-------------------	-------------------	-------------------
-------------------	-------------------	-------------------
-------------------	-------------------	-------------------
-------------------	-------------------	
-------------------	-------------------	

BASKETBALL
(8 terms)

TENNIS
(8 terms)

----

13. FORWARD—REVERSE

This chapter will remind you that every word is a symbol: a word means whatever we agree it means. It will also help you to become sensitive to letter order within words. Notice that there are many three-, four-, and five-letter words that have one meaning when read from left to right, and quite another meaning when read from right to left. The letters STRAW, for example, when read from right to left, become WARTS.

I. In the exercises below, (1) refers to the left-to-right reading, and (2) refers to the right-to-left reading. See how many of the correct letter combinations you can identify.

> *Example:* What word means (1) cooking utensils, and (2) to cease?
> *Answer:* pots—stop

---------- ---------- 1. What word means (1) a spring month, and (2) a sweet potato?

---------- ---------- 2. What word means (1) to jog, and (2) a civil wrong?

---------- ---------- 3. What word means (1) a piece or fraction, and (2) a snare?

---------- ---------- 4. What word means (1) measure of duration, and (2) to send forth?

---------- ---------- 5. What word means (1) a demon, and (2) existed?

---------- ---------- 6. What word means (1) a district of a city, and (2) to sketch?

---------- ---------- 7. What word means (1) a space within four walls, and (2) to secure?

---------- ---------- 8. What word means (1) wicked, and (2) to be alive?

---------- ---------- 9. What word means (1) an entrance, and (2) a crucifix?

---------- ---------- 10. What word means (1) to make merry, and (2) a crowbar?

---------- ---------- 11. What word means (1) an asterisk, and (2) rodents related to mice?

---------- ---------- 12. What word means (1) greedy, and (2) a prima donna?

---------- ---------- 13. What word means (1) to maintain, and (2) to catch a glimpse?

---------- ---------- 14. What word means (1) a strong, low cart, and (2) three feet?

---------- ---------- 15. What word means (1) to encounter, and (2) to swarm?

II. Becoming skillful at it? Here are some more on which to sharpen your wits!

---------- ---------- 1. What word means (1) a worn piece of cloth, and (2) a type of fish?

---------- ---------- 2. What word means (1) a ragout, and (2) moistens?

---------- ---------- 3. What word means (1) existed, and (2) a carpenter's tool?

---------- ---------- 4. What word means (1) except, and (2) a wide, low vessel?

---------- ---------- 5. What word means (1) bridges, and (2) bites sharply at?

---------- ---------- 6. What word means (1) a large saxhorn, and (2) to border on?

---------- ---------- 7. What word means (1) to capture, and (2) to prohibit?

---------- ---------- 8. What word means (1) an aerial maneuver, and (2) a large puddle?

---------- ---------- 9. What word means (1) a hamlet, and (2) a goad?

---------- ---------- 10. What word means (1) skins of fruit, and (2) slumber?

---------- ---------- 11. What word means (1) a stair, and (2) animals kept for pleasure?

---------- ---------- 12. What word means (1) a sailing vessel, and (2) tanks for swimming?

---------- ---------- 13. What word means (1) part of a printed letter, and (2) discharges gunshot?

---------- ---------- 14. What word means (1) glossy, and (2) boat bottoms?

---------- ---------- 15. What word means (1) fitting closely and comfortably, and (2) firearms?

14. REAMS OF RELATIVES

I. Compote. Using apples, lemons, oranges, limes, peaches, grapes, and pineapples, alone or with other words, see how many of the missing words you can supply.

Example: a word meaning "nonsense"
Answer: applesauce

-------------------------------- 1. another name for a tomato (2 words)

-------------------------------- 2. a car that is forever in need of repairs

-------------------------------- 3. an uncle's favorite niece (4 words)

-------------------------------- 4. a pretty girl

-------------------------------- 5. the center of attraction

-------------------------------- 6. an informal method of transmitting information or rumor from person to person

-------------------------------- 7. very good condition (informal, 2 words)

-------------------------------- 8. a kind of lump in the throat (2 words)

-------------------------------- 9. the small cast-iron balls shot from cannon

-------------------------------- 10. a hand grenade made with dynamite (military slang)

II. The World Beyond. Using angels, cherubs, or devils, alone or with other words, see how many of the missing words you can supply.

-------------------------------- 1. the youngest apprentice in a printing office (2 words)

-------------------------------- 2. the financial backer of a play

-------------------------------- 3. a cute baby

-------------------------------- 4. eggs whose yolks have been chopped and mixed with seasoning (2 words)

-------------------------------- 5. a delicate white cake (3 words)

-------------------------------- 6. someone who defends a bad cause (2 words)

-------------------------------- 7. a rich chocolate cake (3 words)

-------------------------------- 8. a dragonfly (3 words)

-------------------------------- 9. spun-glass strands used for Christmas-tree decoration (2 words)

-------------------------------- 10. careless of authority; reckless

15. A ROCKET TO THE MOON

Today is the age of space; tomorrow a vacation on the moon may be a common occurrence. There is still plenty of time to pack your bag, but less time to acquire the special terminology of outer space. How many of the following missing words can you provide? If you miss more than five, you may be condemned forever to vacationing right here on Earth!

The first letter of each answer is given.

g-------------------------------- 1. the Milky Way, for example; also the name of a science-fiction magazine

i-------------------------------- 2. pertaining to travel between Mars and Venus, for example, or between Venus and Earth

a-------------------------------- 3. a traveler outside the atmosphere of the earth

o-------------------------------- 4. the elliptical or curved path around a celestial body

s-------------------------------- 5. a small body, natural or man-made, that revolves around a planet

a-------------------------------- 6. a small starlike planet

c-------------------------------- 7. cup-shaped depressions in the ground, especially on the moon

f-------------------------------- 8. a permanent, man-made satellite, situated to facilitate travel to distant planets (2 words)

g-------------------------------- 9. the force of attraction by which terrestrial bodies tend to fall toward the center of the earth; missing in outer space

l-------------------------------- 10. the site of the take-off of a rocket or spaceship (2 words)

c-------------------------------- 11. the last moments before take-off

s-------------------------------- 12. the gentle "putting down" of a spacecraft or instrument (2 words)

e-------------------------------- 13. in space, movement that takes place outside the spacecraft (2 words)

p-------------------------------- 14. that part of the cargo of a spaceship that is meant to collect information, samples, etc.

d-------------------------------- 15. a reduction in speed, especially when re-entering the earth's atmosphere

l-------------------------------- 16. the distance covered in one year at 186,000 miles a second

t-------------------------------- 17. the curve described by a projectile in its flight through the air

r-------------------------------- 18. a planned meeting of two spacecraft

p-------------------------------- 19. An apogee is the point in the orbit of a moving body most distant from the earth. What is the point nearest the earth called?

d-------------------------------- 20. the physical linking of two spacecraft in space

16. CLIPPED CLUES

Many of our most often used words are really clipped words—or pieces of words. *Advertisement*, for example, is long and awkward; it is easier to say simply *ad*. After a few years the clipped word often becomes a respectable member of our language.

In each sentence below, a blank indicates a missing clipped word. Can you, in each case, identify both the clipped word and the original complete word?

	CLIPPED	ORIGINAL
1. We stopped to buy _____ for our car before we started east.	_____	_____
2. At 8:30 on a June morning Mary reported for her final _____ in biology.	_____	_____
3. My car needed a _____ job.	_____	_____
4. Inflamed throats, aching muscles, and high fevers suggested we were having a _____ epidemic.	_____	_____
5. To get emergency help, one simply picks up the _____ and dials.	_____	_____
6. Children often learn to ride a _____ by using training wheels at first.	_____	_____
7. Most youngsters like to visit the _____ to see the tigers and lions.	_____	_____
8. Your promises, my dear political candidate, are a lot of worthless _____.	_____	_____
9. Energetic and vivacious, she had so much _____ she was immediately chosen as first cheerleader.	_____	_____
10. The criminal, not wishing to be recognized, refused to have his _____ taken.	_____	_____
11. Standing in the rain and sleet, he waved and whistled but had little chance of stopping a _____.	_____	_____
12. With Rover whimpering and yelping from pain, we drove quickly to the _____.	_____	_____

101 Ways to Learn Vocabulary

13. During the World Series a for-
    eigner might well wonder if there
    aren't more baseball _____ in
    this country than there are citizens. _____ _____

14. Man, we had a real wild _____
    play at the dance last night! _____ _____

15. Strong and agile, he liked _____
    better than any of his academic
    subjects. _____ _____

16. With twenty other students I
    waited at the corner for the school
    _____ to pick us up. _____ _____

17. Eager for news of home, he
    dropped a dime at the stand and
    bought an out-of-town _____. _____ _____

18. Before it was torn down, the Sixth
    Avenue _____ was one of the
    cheapest and fastest methods of
    transportation in the city. _____ _____

19. By the secret handshake and the
    Greek letters on his blazer, I knew
    he was a _____ brother. _____ _____

20. After hours of fighting the surf
    and racing on the sand, I devoured
    three _____ with mustard and
    relish. _____ _____

17. ANIMAL LORE

Many animals and insects have helped to name man-made articles and even man's attitudes. On the blank at the left write the name of the animal or insect (and in some cases one more word) to find the word that fits the definition at the right.

Example: a frankfurter
Answer: hot dog

_____	1. a support for work, especially carpentry
_____	2. a tool used for turning nuts
_____	3. to nag, especially to nag one's husband
_____	4. a very brief sleep
_____	5. good, practical common sense
_____	6. rough, boisterous romping
_____	7. a tractor used for hauling or pulling
_____	8. a chopping blow to the back of the neck
_____	9. spiteful; given to petty gossip
_____	10. a tuft of hair, usually standing upright
_____	11. a loud, boisterous laugh
_____	12. a temporary dugout for one or two soldiers
_____	13. a derisive cry, sometimes used by audiences
_____	14. a caper or antic; any ludicrous tomfoolery
_____	15. a ranch hand in charge of ranging cattle
_____	16. a tool used by a plumber and named after a reptile
_____	17. a rather pungent condiment
_____	18. a gathering of friends or neighbors for work
_____	19. shy; bashful
_____	20. describing a book having the corners of the pages bent back

18. ANIMALS ARE FAIR GAME!

There are almost as many names for groups of animals as there are names for animals. For each animal listed below, write the "group" word that is appropriate. For example, _____ of elephants should be *herd* of elephants. If you can identify correctly the first 40 of the group names, you are certainly a genius! (Duplicates are occasionally possible.)

1. _____ of fish
2. _____ of dogs
3. _____ of birds
4. _____ of quail
5. _____ of bees
6. _____ of lions
7. _____ of partridges
8. _____ of whales
9. _____ of swine
10. _____ of sardines
11. _____ of nightingales
12. _____ of buffalo
13. _____ of cottontails
14. _____ of rhinoceroses
15. _____ of porpoises

16. _____ of sheep
17. _____ of mules
18. _____ of apes
19. _____ of ants
20. _____ of wolves
21. _____ of locusts
22. _____ of larks
23. _____ of geese
24. _____ of chicks
25. _____ of storks
26. _____ of turkeys
27. _____ of rabbits
28. _____ of curs
29. _____ of jellyfish
30. _____ of eggs

The next ten are seldom used except by specialists. Can you guess *any* of them?

31. _____ of leopards
32. _____ of hogs
33. _____ of jackrabbits
34. _____ of bears
35. _____ of wildcats

36. _____ of starlings
37. _____ of pheasants
38. _____ of colts
39. _____ of turtledoves
40. _____ of woodcock

The last ten are for the two-legged animal!

41. _____ of people
42. _____ of worshippers
43. _____ of hoodlums
44. _____ of sailors
45. _____ of actors

46. _____ of editors
47. _____ of angels
48. _____ of teachers
49. _____ of characters
50. _____ of maidens

19. BATTLE OF THE SEXES

I. Wherever there is a male, there is a female—and vice versa! For each of the masculine terms given below, give the feminine equivalent:

1. duke _____
2. czar _____
3. earl _____
4. marquis _____
5. sultan _____

6. alumnus _____
7. widower _____
8. executor _____
9. wizard _____
10. postmaster _____

II. For each male animal given below, give the female equivalent:

1. drake _____
2. fox _____
3. peacock _____
4. buck _____
5. tomcat _____

6. stallion _____
7. ram _____
8. stag _____
9. rooster _____
10. gander _____

20. KNOW YOUR OWN CHILD!

When a human being gives birth to its young, we call the baby (among other things!) a child. But what is the offspring of a cat called . . . or of a goat? Try your hand at the following quiz, writing after the name of each animal the term commonly used for its offspring. If you are any kind of zoologist at all, you should be able to come up with 16 to 20 correct answers. If your score ranges between 10 and 15, you are average. If you score below 10, you are no friend to the animal world!

1. cat	_____	11. hare	_____
2. goat	_____	12. kangaroo	_____
3. horse	_____	13. goose	_____
4. bear	_____	14. eagle	_____
5. whale	_____	15. lion	_____
6. sheep	_____	16. swan	_____
7. hog	_____	17. beaver	_____
8. seal	_____	18. fox	_____
9. wolf	_____	19. frog	_____
10. deer	_____	20. salmon	_____

Part V. *Word Games*

People have been playing games from the dawn of human history. Probably the caveman and his wife had their own favorite "parlor" games for the long winter evenings. But it is only in our own time that game-playing has become a respectable means of acquiring scientific and historical information. It can be useful, too, in enriching your vocabulary.

The twenty word games that follow have been developed to help you gain skill in letter manipulation and word handling. Of the raw materials— words—there is a varied and almost endless supply. As you play these games, you will find you are growing more and more curious about words, that your vocabulary is increasing rapidly, and that your writing is gaining accuracy and power.

Best of all, while you are mastering all of these skills, you will be having fun—learning games that can brighten an auto trip, enliven a party, or make tolerable an otherwise intolerably dull meeting!

1. CASUAL CROSSWORDS

Crossword puzzles are a national pastime—international, too. Commuters do them on the way to and from work. People waiting for appointments do them. Young people, middle-aged people, and old people do them. Truck drivers and Presidents do them. Do you?

If you have never tackled a crossword puzzle, try a few of these "casual crosswords." Let's look at the first one below. Begin by glancing over the definitions. Choose one that looks easy. You probably can guess the correct word for #2 Down—an inhabitant of heaven. *Angel*, of course. Write the letters in the squares, starting with the #2 square. Now use these letters as aids in finding other words. #2 Across is a drink similar to beer. You now know that it is a three-letter word beginning with "a". This should help you to think of *ale*. Continue, following the same procedure. You will soon be able to complete a "casual crossword" in a few minutes.

I.

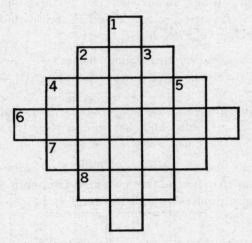

ACROSS	DOWN
2. a drink similar to beer	1. fine or luxurious in dress
4. a wing of a building (two words: article plus noun)	2. an inhabitant of heaven
6. to propose	3. to choose by vote
7. to respond to a stimulus	4. the first three letters of a prefix meaning gold
8. less news today (abbr.)	5. a kind of ship

101 Ways to Learn Vocabulary

II.

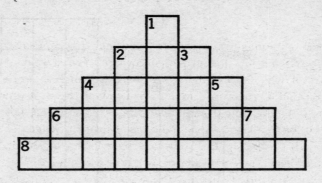

ACROSS

2. a legendary bird
4. an adult male voice
6. the least possible
8. the favored type of government in the U.S.

DOWN

1. pertaining to sound
2. a marketplace for divorce
3. the first four letters of synonym for "friend" (_ _ _ _ ade)
4. In Dickens' *Christmas Carol*, he is called "Tiny."
5. road under Asia (abbr.)
6. a personal pronoun, objective case
7. master of ceremonies (abbr.)

III.

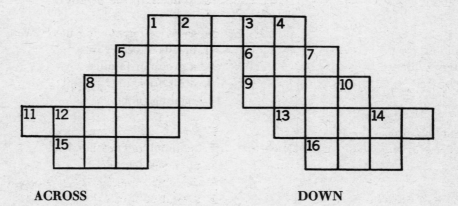

ACROSS

1. suspension of consciousness
5. an American poet and short story writer
6. a negative adverb
8. gelid
9. descending direction
11. a large animal of the deer family
13. disturbance of the peace (pl.)
15. to change the color of
16. a couple

DOWN

1. only
2. guided
3. terminate
4. indigent
5. an attitude or posture
7. to taunt; to gibe at
8. shy; modest
10. at the present time
12. olive drab (abbr.)
14. preposition

IV.

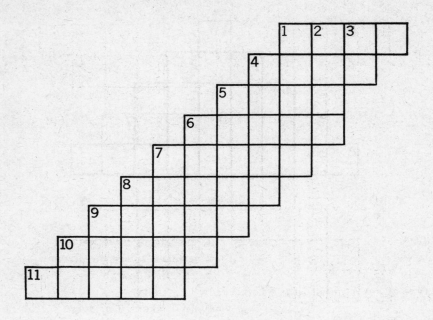

ACROSS

1. form of address to a woman of rank
4. a group of three persons
5. wholesome
6. to come to an end
7. attire
8. seashore
9. apart from others
10. to frighten suddenly
11. opposite of "closes"

DOWN

1. waste matter; refuse
2. an assistant
3. modus operandi (abbr.)
4. to drink to the health of
5. web-footed birds
6. a device for moving heavy weights
7. means of access (pl.)
8. a group of families
9. a highly skilled person
10. spelling (abbr.)

101 Ways to Learn Vocabulary

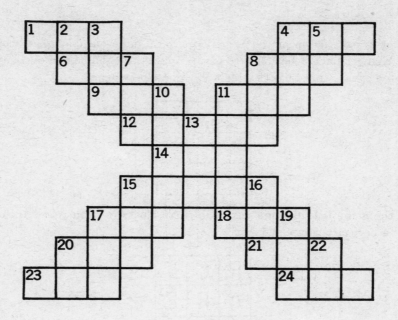

ACROSS

1. a rocky hill
4. amount (abbr.)
6. past tense of "dig"
8. to snoop
9. to command
11. a small child
12. very cold
14. a small rug
15. rustic
17. a mongrel dog
18. to bow the head
20. to prevent from speaking
21. something spun by spiders
23. to drink a little
24. damp

DOWN

2. officer of the day (abbr.)
3. to exert friction
4. the study of painting, drawing, and sculpture
5. possessive form of a personal pronoun
7. a type of boat
8. a seedcase
10. to make an objection
11. Hyperion, for example
13. a Roman god
15. a carpet
16. to moo
17. a type of head covering
19. moisture, especially in early morning
20. a U.S. soldier (slang)
22. exist

Don't stop now! Almost every newspaper has a daily crossword puzzle. Try these. You will find them entertaining and challenging. And your vocabulary will improve as if by magic!

2. "SQUARE" WORDS

This word game is a variation of the Word Square, a game old enough to be listed in today's dictionaries. A few changes have been made to permit greater flexibility and challenge.

Just begin with a square three blocks wide and three blocks deep:

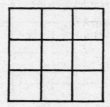

The object of the game is to position letters in these blocks to form words both horizontally and vertically. Below is a perfectly completed square.

```
R O T
A R E
P E N
```

Now see if you can find different three-letter words to complete the following two squares:

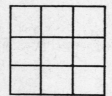

Successful? Good. Now look at this completed 4-x-4 square.

```
M A T E
I R O N
L E N D
L A S S
```

Harder, isn't it? Can you complete these 4-x-4 squares?

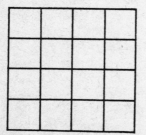

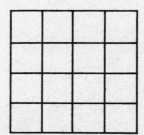

101 Ways to Learn Vocabulary

You are ready now for the classic—the 5-x-5 blocked square. Here is an example:

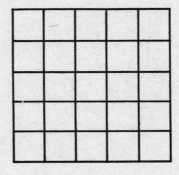

This is *really* hard. Challenge yourself to complete the one below.

You are now ready to play the game with a friend. Read the rules below; then play your first round.

1. Each player should block out a square on a sheet of paper.
2. Player A selects one letter—perhaps "t." Each player inserts the "t" in any one of his blocks.
3. Player B chooses the next letter. This time it could be an "a." Each writes the "a" in any block desired.
4. The above procedure continues until all the blocks are filled.
5. Each player figures his score (see the sample square following). The player who has the higher score wins.

Example:

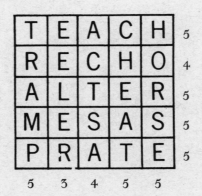

Note that the second horizontal line counts 4 points for the word *echo*; the second vertical line counts 3 points for the word *eel*. Plurals and colloquialisms may be used, but not proper nouns and foreign words. For the above square, the score would be 46.

A clue for you: As you insert the first letters into the square, have in mind possible five-letter words for the first horizontal and the first vertical lines. This will get you off to a good start.

3. PYRAMID PLAY

Here is a game that will extend your vocabulary and develop your awareness of word structure at the same time. Play it graphically—on a blackboard or on scrap paper.

1. Build a pyramid of words, using the eight clues given below. All the words needed to complete this pyramid begin and end with the letter "d."

$$— — —$$
$$— — — —$$
$$— — — — —$$
$$— — — — — —$$
$$— — — — — — —$$
$$— — — — — — — —$$
$$— — — — — — — — —$$
$$— — — — — — — — — —$$

1st line: a three-letter word meaning "accomplished"
2nd line: a four-letter word meaning "came to the end of its life"
3rd line: a five-letter word meaning "freed from moisture"
4th line: a six-letter word meaning "placed between two piers"
5th line: a seven-letter word meaning "emptied of all liquid"
6th line: an eight-letter word meaning "claimed as a right"
7th line: a nine-letter word meaning "perceived"
8th line: a ten-letter word meaning "found out," "learned"

2. Now try this one. All words begin and end with "s."

$$— — — —$$
$$— — — — —$$
$$— — — — — —$$
$$— — — — — — —$$
$$— — — — — — — —$$
$$— — — — — — — — —$$
$$— — — — — — — — — —$$

1st line: plural of a tool used by carpenters
2nd line: plural meaning reservoirs or pits for fluids
3rd line: plural meaning tubes for sucking up a beverage
4th line: plural meaning rivulets, or brooks
5th line: plural for hinged covers for windows
6th line: plural meaning paved pathways
7th line: plural for something offered up as a religious act

3. This one should help stretch your vocabulary. All words begin and end with "m":

<pre>
              _ _ _
             _ _ _ _
            _ _ _ _ _
           _ _ _ _ _ _
          _ _ _ _ _ _ _
         _ _ _ _ _ _ _ _
        _ _ _ _ _ _ _ _ _
       _ _ _ _ _ _ _ _ _ _
</pre>

1st line: silent
2nd line: to cripple
3rd line: an expression of a general truth; a proverb
4th line: a building for housing art or scientific specimens
5th line: the least allowable
6th line: impetus, as of a moving body
7th line: a piece of machinery
8th line: a tobacco pipe with a carved, claylike bowl

4. On this pyramid, all words begin and end with "r":

<pre>
              _ _ _ _
             _ _ _ _ _
            _ _ _ _ _ _
           _ _ _ _ _ _ _
          _ _ _ _ _ _ _ _
         _ _ _ _ _ _ _ _ _
        _ _ _ _ _ _ _ _ _ _
</pre>

1st line: to rise up on the hind legs
2nd line: a device for finding an object by radio waves
3rd line: bitter resentment
4th line: normal; usual
5th line: a device to heat air
6th line: an official recorder
7th line: one who rejects

5. On this one, all words begin and end in "t":

$$- - -$$
$$- - - -$$
$$- - - - -$$
$$- - - - - -$$
$$- - - - - - -$$
$$- - - - - - - -$$
$$- - - - - - - - -$$
$$- - - - - - - - - -$$

1st line: to make lace
2nd line: a small cluster of hairs
3rd line: an appointed meeting
4th line: a small tower
5th line: a violent stream
6th line: early evening
7th line: temporary; not lasting
8th line: an inexperienced person

4. FROM ONE, MANY!

One of the most popular word games is also the easiest to play anywhere. It requires only pencil and paper. Begin by selecting a fairly simple word. Write this word at the top of your sheet of paper. Now make as many words as possible from the original word, following these rules:

1. Use only the letters in the original word. Letters may be omitted, but they may not be added.
2. Use each letter only as often as it appears in the original word.
3. Past tenses and plurals may not be used.
4. Arrange the words you make up in initial letter groups.
5. If two or more players are playing the game, anyone who questions the existence of a word given by another player may challenge it and consult the dictionary.

Sample word: STUDENT

den	end	net	send	ten	us
dent		nest	set	tent	use
dust		nude	sun	tend	
dun		nut	sue	test	
dune			stet	tune	
duet			stun	tun	
due			stud		
			stunt		

Some helpful hints:

1. Remember that some consonants pair off as initial sounds, e.g., "st." This leads to "stun," "stud," and "stunt."
2. Remember that some consonants pair off as final sounds, e.g., "st." This leads to "dust," "nest," and "test."
3. Try rhymes. "Sun" may lead you to "dun" and "tun."

Now try the same procedure on other words.
Try these variations:

1. How many words beginning with a vowel (a, e, i, o, u) can you create from *education*? (Aim for twenty words.)

----

2. How many four-letter words can you create from *gentleman*? (Aim for twenty-five words.)

----

101 Ways to Learn Vocabulary

3. How many nouns (name-words) can you create from *philatelist*? (Aim for twenty-five words.)

----

4. Challenge some friends to see who can make the longest list of words from a word such as *serendipity*.

----

5. ADD-A-LETTER

For this word game, you will need your own dictionary. The rules are simple; the playing is not. From each word on the list, form a second word by *adding one letter*. This letter may be added at the end of the word, at the beginning, or in the middle. Here are a couple of easy examples to get you started. From the word "can," you can make "scan" by adding an "s" at the beginning, "clan" by inserting an "l," or "cane" by adding an "e" at the end. From "rip" you can develop "trip" or "ripe." (Plurals not allowed.)

I. Can you make at least one new word from each of the following by using the "add-a-letter" method?

1. bit	_ _ _ _ _ _ _ _ _ _ _ _ _	11. demur	_ _ _ _ _ _ _ _ _ _ _ _
2. tin	_ _ _ _ _ _ _ _ _ _ _ _ _	12. eight	_ _ _ _ _ _ _ _ _ _ _ _
3. ask	_ _ _ _ _ _ _ _ _ _ _ _ _	13. wave	_ _ _ _ _ _ _ _ _ _ _ _
4. one	_ _ _ _ _ _ _ _ _ _ _ _ _	14. canon	_ _ _ _ _ _ _ _ _ _ _ _
5. den	_ _ _ _ _ _ _ _ _ _ _ _ _	15. ordnance	_ _ _ _ _ _ _ _ _ _ _ _
6. oak	_ _ _ _ _ _ _ _ _ _ _ _ _	16. flaming	_ _ _ _ _ _ _ _ _ _ _ _
7. cane	_ _ _ _ _ _ _ _ _ _ _ _ _	17. statue	_ _ _ _ _ _ _ _ _ _ _ _
8. lass	_ _ _ _ _ _ _ _ _ _ _ _ _	18. venal	_ _ _ _ _ _ _ _ _ _ _ _
9. print	_ _ _ _ _ _ _ _ _ _ _ _ _	19. piece	_ _ _ _ _ _ _ _ _ _ _ _
10. rein	_ _ _ _ _ _ _ _ _ _ _ _ _	20. plaster	_ _ _ _ _ _ _ _ _ _ _ _

II. Now see if, with the help of definitions, you can go one step further—to add a letter and make a new word, and then to add a second letter and make a second new word.

Example:

RAT   _ _ _ _ RATE _ _ _ _   _ _ _ GRATE _ _ _
         (payment, price)   (to rub against)

1. AID   _ _ _ _ _ _ _ _ _ _ _   _ _ _ _ _ _ _ _ _ _ _
              (commented)   (sober, sedate)

2. ASH   _ _ _ _ _ _ _ _ _ _ _   _ _ _ _ _ _ _ _ _ _
         (a mixture, a jumble)   (severe)

3. TOR   _ _ _ _ _ _ _ _ _ _   _ _ _ _ _ _ _ _ _ _
                (ripped)   (a prickle, a spine)

4. LAD   _ _ _ _ _ _ _ _ _ _   _ _ _ _ _ _ _ _ _ _
            (happy, pleased)   (a grassy space)

5. REAM   _ _ _ _ _ _ _ _ _ _   _ _ _ _ _ _ _ _ _ _
            (the choicest part)   (to cry out)

6. READ   _ _ _ _ _ _ _ _ _ _   _ _ _ _ _ _ _ _ _ _
                (to walk)   (a thin filament)

7. LET   ------------   ------------
            (opposite of right)   (divided, split)

8. EON   ------------   ------------
             (a laborer)   (a type of flower)

9. SAVE   ------------   ------------
        (a stick, a cudgel)   (to perish with hunger)

10. PART   ------------   ------------
      (a political group)   (equality)

6. CHANGE-A-LETTER

If you enjoyed Add-a-Letter, you will be even more challenged by "Change-a-Letter." This time, instead of adding a letter to the original word, change one letter to another. For example, if you start with the word *class*, you can change "c" to "g" to make *glass*.

I. See if you can make one new word from each of the following by changing one letter.

1. bath	_____	11. simple	_____
2. plan	_____	12. present	_____
3. read	_____	13. fragrant	_____
4. treat	_____	14. spacious	_____
5. patch	_____	15. hideout	_____
6. clamp	_____	16. errand	_____
7. level	_____	17. turbid	_____
8. bacon	_____	18. faker	_____
9. idiot	_____	19. hammock	_____
10. incense	_____	20. flower	_____

II. Now see if, with the help of definitions, you can go one step further—to change a letter and make a new word, and then to change a second letter and make a second new word.

Example:

BOARD   ___ BEARD ___   ___ HEARD ___
              (hair on the chin)   (listened)

1. TERSE   _____   _____
                        (taut)   (stupid)

2. STILL   _____   _____
          (steps for passing over a fence)   (not fresh)

3. ROUND   _____   _____
                    (a hillock)   (to go up)

4. BRAKE   _____   _____
                  (a male duck)   (a curtain)

5. RATHER   _____   _____
          (a thin slice of bacon)   (a flat metal or leather ring)

6. LARGE   _____   _____
          (an unpowered vessel)   (a mark or emblem)

7. HAMMER   _____   _____
                    (to hinder)   (to meddle)

8. BARBER   _____   _____
                    (to trade)   (playful teasing)

9. MANTLE - - - - - - - - - - - -   - - - - - - - - - - - -
              (to crush or disfigure)   (to hang loosely)

10. RECENT - - - - - - - - - - - -   - - - - - - - - - - - -
              (to disavow a former belief)   (to pour off without
                                               disturbing the sediment)

7. CHANGE-ABOUT

Before you try this game, you should be an expert at Add-a-Letter and Change-a-Letter. For Change-About you must be really skillful at manipulating letters. Begin with Step I, which deals with simple letter manipulation.

Step I. Change the first word into the last word by changing one letter at a time. Do not, however, change the order of the letters.

> *Example: bait* to *tell* (4 steps)
> *Answer:* bait—bai*l*—*t*ail—ta*l*l—t*e*ll

Now try these:

1. *book* to *leap* (5 steps) _____
2. *grow* to *slim* (6 steps) _____
3. *word* to *sane* (5 steps) _____
4. *rose* to *cart* (5 steps) _____
5. *vase* to *pink* (5 steps) _____
6. *take* to *live* (4 steps) _____
7. *play* to *flea* (5 steps) _____
8. *sane* to *link* (5 steps) _____
9. *draw* to *prop* (4 steps) _____
10. *bore* to *fold* (4 steps) _____

Now proceed to Step II.

Step II. Change one letter in the first word to make the second word, one letter in the second to make the third, etc. The definitions should be helpful.

1. *a.* STAMP

   b. _____ a rascal

   c. _____ a steep slope

   d. _____ to frighten

   e. _____ apportion

   f. _____ a county in Great Britain

2. *a.* CRAVE

   b. _____ a large wading bird

   c. _____ a grouchy person

   d. _____ a trick

101 Ways to Learn Vocabulary

e. ---------- a piece of timber

f. ---------- the side of an animal

3. *a.* PIPER

 b. ---------- material on which we write

 c. ---------- one who sets the rate of movement

 d. ---------- a cutter for smoothing a surface

 e. ---------- a swindler

 f. ---------- a Hindu ascetic

4. *a.* BRAND

 b. ---------- to weave together

 c. ---------- The cerebrum is one part.

 d. ---------- well-developed muscles

 e. ---------- a dark color

 f. ---------- fully matured

5. *a.* GREAT

 b. ---------- to deal with

 c. ---------- to step

 d. ---------- to fear greatly

 e. ---------- images occurring during sleep

 f. ---------- the best part of anything

8. WIT-TWISTERS

Our next game is "borrowed." For some time it has been a weekly feature in the *Saturday Review*. Playing this game will have a twofold reward: (1) You will gain in skill in manipulating letters and words, and (2) you may wish to seek out other issues of the *Saturday Review* for more Wit-Twisters, thus becoming acquainted with this provocative periodical.

Here are the rules and a sample Wit-Twister, as given by Arthur Swan, editor of the feature.

The object of the game is to complete the poem by thinking of one word whose letters, when rearranged, will yield the appropriate word for each series of blanks. Each dash within a blank corresponds to a letter of the word. Now try this Wit-Twister:

Good landlord, fill the flowing _ _ _ _

Until their _ _ _ _ run over!

Tonight, we'll _ _ _ _ upon this _ _ _ _ ;

Tomorrow, _ _ _ _ for Dover!

(*Answers:* pots, tops, stop, spot, post.)

Below are three more Wit-Twisters that you might like to try. Dozens more may be found in any library in back issues of the *Saturday Review*.

1. In a _ _ _ _ _ dozed the medium, muttering low,

   "Imps sprout from my flesh! Just feel the _ _ _ _ _ grow!"

   But the psychic researcher was not taken in

   By the unripened _ _ _ _ _ that were taped to her skin.
   (October 21, 1967)

2. That _ _ _ _ _ parson, whose mien seems meek,

   Whose _ _ _ _ _ are modest, and whose cheek

   Says, "Smite me if ye will, ye vermin,"

   _ _ _ _ _ us weekly with his sermon.
   (July 22, 1967)

3. The moon was but a _ _ _ _ _ _ thin;

   No _ _ _ _ _ _ light its spare arc gave.

   The ghoul lured weary people in,

   And munched their _ _ _ _ _ _ in his cave.
   (September 23, 1967)

Possible follow-up: You might like to try your hand at writing an original Wit-Twister. If you do, here is one tip: the letter "s" is almost essential to success!

9. SCRAMBLED WORDS

I. Here is a variation of the old anagram game. Can you unscramble each of the following words so that a real word emerges? Each scrambled word is followed by two hints to help you in unscrambling.

    1. HECOS   _____
        Hints: *a.* It means "selected."
              b. Remember that the letters "ch" often go together.

    2. ENUQE   _____
        Hints: *a.* Remember that the letters "qu" always go together.
              b. It refers to a person of royal rank.

    3. KLABE   _____
        Hints: *a.* The first letter is "b."
              b. It means bare and desolate.

    4. NUCED   _____
        Hints: *a.* It names a dull-witted student.
              b. It ends with the letter "e."

    5. BOHAPI   _____
        Hints: *a.* Remember that the letters "ph" often go together.
              b. It may be defined as an obsessive fear.

II. Now try your wits on the following scrambled words. This time only one hint is given for each word.

    1. LANIE   _____   (Hint: a complete stranger)

    2. DAIR   _____   (Hint: dry or barren)

    3. BLIG   _____   (Hint: fluent)

    4. BROOT   _____   (Hint: a mechanical man)

    5. PLIMY   _____   (Hint: suggest indirectly)

III. Follow exactly the same procedure as before, with these more difficult words.

    1. BRYDIH   _____   (Hint: of mixed origin)

    2. CLUREES   _____   (Hint: a hermit)

    3. GEARIM   _____   (Hint: an optical illusion)

    4. SPENDIT   _____   (Hint: a fixed payment for services)

    5. SOACH   _____   (Hint: complete confusion)

IV. Here is a final challenging version of scrambled words. In each sentence one word is underlined and one word is omitted. The omitted word will be implied by the context and will be made up of the same letters as those in the underlined word. Your task, of course, is to try to figure out what word has been omitted.

Example: Learning by rote frustrated him so much that he _ _ _ _ _ _ up his books.

Answer: tore

Now here are some sentences on which you can sharpen your intellectual teeth!

1. After being found guilty of pirating the plane, he was sentenced to a long term in a _ _ _ _ _ _ _ _ _ _ _ _ _ _ colony.

2. In studying the role of Paul Bunyan, the actor learned a good deal of folk _ _ _ _ _ _ _ _ _ _ _ _ _ _.

3. Since it was getting late and I had to be up early, I put the mystery _ _ _ _ _ _ _ _ _ _ _ _ _ back on the bookshelf.

4. After placing his masterpiece in the kiln, the sculptor felt he had forged one more _ _ _ _ _ _ _ _ _ _ _ _ _ in the chain to success.

5. His _ _ _ _ _ _ _ _ _ _ _ _ _ failed; he had been sure of winning, but his trickery was spotted by the judges.

6. To awaken his _ _ _ _ _ _ _ _ _ _ _ _ _ talent, Maria challenged her husband to write a novel better than the one he had just reviewed.

7. The _ _ _ _ _ _ _ _ _ _ _ _ _ winds seemed to freeze him to the bone as he began to glide across the ice.

8. In Hades the _ _ _ _ _ _ _ _ _ _ _ _ _ of Achilles whimpered.

9. The marshal poses as a rancher while he is secretly organizing a _ _ _ _ _ _ _ _ _ _ _ _ _.

10. "What does sprout mean?" In his _ _ _ _ _ _ _ _ _ _ _ _ _ the sleepy student could not remember the correct answer.

11. As was his _ _ _ _ _ _ _ _ _ _ _ _ _, he went to town on Sunday afternoon.

12. The trio, the idols of the teen-agers, were horrified to find themselves in the middle of a violent _ _ _ _ _ _ _ _ _ _ _ _ _.

13. It requires no great mental ability to _ _ _ _ _ _ _ _ _ _ _ _ _ the current popularization of aggressive behavior.

14. In New Mexico he lived in an abode that is commonly described as _ _ _ _ _ _ _ _ _ _ _ _ _.

15. If you discern a difference in quality between the two rugs, you can _ _ _ _ _ _ _ _ _ _ _ _ _ your order.

Follow-up: Make up some sentences using similar pairs of words and try them on your friends.

10. DOUBLE TROUBLE

I. This game is just for fun. Some words in English have been formed by simply doubling the first syllable or syllables. See how many you can identify.

Example: child's name for the maternal parent
Answer: mama

-------------------- 1. a hard substance deposited on teeth

-------------------- 2. a native drum

-------------------- 3. a ballet skirt

-------------------- 4. a bloodsucking fly

-------------------- 5. a low, continuous sound

-------------------- 6. a disease caused by a deficiency of vitamin B_1

-------------------- 7. a piece of soft, coated candy

-------------------- 8. a dance popular in Paris in the 1830's

-------------------- 9. a clumsy, flightless bird, now extinct

-------------------- 10. a type of toy

-------------------- 11. slang for antiaircraft fire

-------------------- 12. a yeast-raised cake, flavored with rum

-------------------- 13. a rustling of silk

-------------------- 14. an adjective describing something mediocre, something neither very good nor very bad

-------------------- 15. a long, loose dress that falls free from the shoulders; originally Hawaiian

II. Other expressions—often casual, even colloquial—have been formed by "doubling with a difference," that is, repeating a word with one letter changed. Try your skill on these picturesque words.

Example: a game of table tennis
Answer: pingpong

-------------------------- 1. a combined radio transmitter and receiver

-------------------------- 2. trimming made of narrow zigzag braid

-------------------------- 3. originally, an Indian ceremony; now a conference

-------------------------- 4. meaningless incantation or ritual

-------------------------- 5. a hodgepodge; a jumble

-------------------------- 6. to be irresolute

-------------------------- 7. gossip

-------------------------- 8. trickery; jugglery

-------------------------- 9. short and plumply round

-------------------------- 10. worthless people; rabble

-------------------------- 11. having a monotonous cadence or rhythm

-------------------------- 12. a trinket

-------------------------- 13. a barrel organ, played by turning a crank

-------------------------- 14. colloquially, a very important person

-------------------------- 15. to trick; to deceive

11. PALINDROMES

A *palindrome* is a word or phrase that reads the same backward or forward. Here are a few simple ones:

boob	noon	refer
rotor	eve	redder
ere	peep	pep
deed	sees	pop

Can you think of single-word palindromes that fit the following definitions:

_ _ _ _ _ _ _ _ _ _   1. an electronic device to determine the presence of an object

_ _ _ _ _ _ _ _ _ _   2. pertaining to a city or to citizenship

_ _ _ _ _ _ _ _ _ _   3. even, flat, smooth

_ _ _ _ _ _ _ _ _ _   4. an opinion or principle held as true

_ _ _ _ _ _ _ _ _ _   5. something very minute

Now try to supply two-word palindromes for the following descriptions:

> *Example:* pierce flying mammals
> *Answer:*   stab bats ("Pierce" means "stab," and bats are flying mammals.)

_ _ _ _ _ _ _ _ _ _ _ _ _ _ _   6. a royal beer

_ _ _ _ _ _ _ _ _ _ _ _ _ _ _   7. a dull poet

_ _ _ _ _ _ _ _ _ _ _ _ _ _ _   8. an eager prima donna

_ _ _ _ _ _ _ _ _ _ _ _ _ _ _   9. a talkfest on many topics

_ _ _ _ _ _ _ _ _ _ _ _ _ _ _   10. a place to buy a trolley in London

Three-word palindromes such as the following are much more challenging:

> Midday command to a tired person: "'Tis noon; sit."

Can you create your own three-word palindrome?

Finally, here are two questions answered by full-sentence palindromes:

> *Question* (asked by Eve of Adam): "Who are you?"
> *Answer:* "Madam, I'm Adam."

> *Question:* What was Napoleon's complaint after he saw Elba, his place of exile?
> *Answer:* "Able was I ere I saw Elba."

Full-sentence palindromes such as these well-known examples are exceedingly difficult to create. Trying to create them, however, is good mental exercise! Why not try to make up one of your own?

12. ALLITERATION, ANYONE?

Most people enjoy alliteration. Alliteration is the repetition of the initial *sound* in two or more neighboring words. "The *seven sisters swam swiftly* down the *silvery stream*" is an example of alliteration carried to excess. Used moderately, however, alliteration can be effective—in letters, in speeches, even in conversation.

Sharpen your alliterative sense by playing the following games.

I. Provide each of the following subjects with an alliterative verb:

Example: The child _ _ _ _ _ _.
Answer: You might insert *chuckled, cheered, cheated,* or *chanted.* All four begin with the "ch" sound that begins the word "child," and all four make sense. A child really might chuckle, cheer, cheat, or chant!

1. The boy _ _ _ _ _ _ _ _ _ _ _ _ _ _ _ _ _.
2. The girl _ _ _ _ _ _ _ _ _ _ _ _ _ _ _ _ _.
3. The man _ _ _ _ _ _ _ _ _ _ _ _ _ _ _ _ _.
4. The woman _ _ _ _ _ _ _ _ _ _ _ _ _ _ _ _.
5. The baby _ _ _ _ _ _ _ _ _ _ _ _ _ _ _ _ _.

II. Provide each of the following adjectives with an alliterative noun:

Example: a jeering _ _ _ _ _ _
Answer: You might insert *jockey, jailer,* or *joker.*

1. a dancing _ _ _ _ _ _ _ _ _ _ _ _ _ _ _ _
2. a grotesque _ _ _ _ _ _ _ _ _ _ _ _ _ _ _
3. a hysterical _ _ _ _ _ _ _ _ _ _ _ _ _ _ _
4. a scathing _ _ _ _ _ _ _ _ _ _ _ _ _ _ _
5. a tedious _ _ _ _ _ _ _ _ _ _ _ _ _ _ _

III. Provide each of the following nouns with an alliterative adjective:

Example: a _ _ _ _ _ _ panther
Answer: You might insert *playful, pampered, pale,* or *peaceful.*

1. a _ _ _ _ _ _ _ _ _ _ _ _ _ _ _ _ stream
2. a _ _ _ _ _ _ _ _ _ _ _ _ _ _ _ _ melody
3. a _ _ _ _ _ _ _ _ _ _ _ _ _ _ _ _ day
4. a _ _ _ _ _ _ _ _ _ _ _ _ _ _ _ _ war
5. a _ _ _ _ _ _ _ _ _ _ _ _ _ _ _ _ voter

IV. Provide each of the following verbs with an alliterative adverb:

> *Example:* She spoke _ _ _ _ _ _.
> *Answer:* You might insert *sadly*, *sweetly*, *slowly*, or *suddenly*.

1. She cried _.

2. He fought _.

3. He lived _.

4. She performed _.

5. He ran _.

13. ONE WORMY WOMBAT

Here's a fresh and funny game of alliteration that demands a dash of imagination and some skillful searching in the dictionary.

First, let us set the stage. The March hare, King Midas, and Jack Sprat are giving a dinner party. As their ten guests, eccentrics all, arrive, each places his order. Consider yourself each of the ten guests in turn. As guest #1, you order "one wormy wombat."

As guest #2, you might order "two tender terrapin."

As guest #3, "three thrumming thrushes."

As guest #4, "four fricasseed foxes," etc.

Note that alliteration involves *sound*, not necessarily initial letters. Thus, "one" and "wormy" are alliterative, but "knight" and "king" are not. Note also that the order you will place includes three words: a number, an adjective, and a food or possible source of food.

Now march into the dinner party and give your order loud and clear:

"I order . . ."

one   ---------------------- ---------------------- .

two   ---------------------- ---------------------- .

three   ---------------------- ---------------------- .

four   ---------------------- ---------------------- .

five   ---------------------- ---------------------- .

six   ---------------------- ---------------------- .

seven   ---------------------- ---------------------- .

eight   ---------------------- ---------------------- .

nine   ---------------------- ---------------------- .

ten   ---------------------- ---------------------- .

Variation: At dinner parties, in addition to eating, you meet all kinds of people. Use the same alliterative technique to describe some of the fascinating people at the party. Begin with "I met . . ."

one   ---------willowy-------- ---------woman-------- .

two   ---------------------- ---------------------- .

three   ---------------------- ---------------------- .

four   ---------------------- ---------------------- .

five   ---------------------- ---------------------- .

six   ---------------------- ---------------------- .

seven   ---------------------- ---------------------- .

eight   ---------------------- ---------------------- .

nine   ---------------------- ---------------------- .

ten   ---------------------- ---------------------- .

14. RHYME-TIME

Almost everyone has a natural delight in rhyme. Interestingly enough, rhymes can be used to sharpen your word sense and to improve your pronunciation.

I. Start with simple lists. If someone asked you to list five words that rhyme with *at*, you would have no trouble in thinking of *bat*, *cat*, *fat*, *mat*, and *rat*. "Warm up" by listing five words that rhyme with each of the words below. (Check every letter in the alphabet. Don't forget double initial consonants as, for example, those in *flat* and *brat*.)

1. AM   2. CRIME   3. BITE

------------   ------------   ------------

------------   ------------   ------------

------------   ------------   ------------

------------   ------------   ------------

------------   ------------   ------------

II. Now try a guessing game that is based on rhymes. If you play this with a friend, one of you should take the part of Player A, the other the part of Player B. But you can play it alone, taking both parts.

Example:

(A) I know a word that rhymes with *goat*. (If two people play, Player A should have a specific word in mind.)

(B) Is it a vehicle for water transportation?

(A) No, it is not a _____. (Insert the word that names a vehicle for water transportation and that rhymes with *goat—boat*, of course.)

(B) Is it an article of clothing?

(A) No, it is not a _____. (*coat*)

(B) Is it something that Ivory soap can do?

(A) No, it is not _____. (*float*)

(B) Is it a defensive ditch around a castle?

(A) Yes, it is a _____. (*moat*)

Do you get the idea? Then, try these:

1. (A) I know a word that rhymes with *grade*.
   (B) Is it the business of buying and selling?

   (A) No, it is not _____.
   (B) Is it the flat, cutting part of a knife?

   (A) No, it is not a _____.
   (B) Is it a young girl?

   (A) No, it is not a _____.

(B) Is it a tool used for digging?

(A) Yes, it is a _ _ _ _ _ _ _ _ _ _ .

(Note that if two people are playing, Player B may come up with the right word on the first guess.)

2. (A) I know a word that rhymes with *mate*.
(B) Is it the top of one's head?

(A) No, it is not a _ _ _ _ _ _ _ _ _ _ .
(B) Is it a country or nation?

(A) No, it is not a _ _ _ _ _ _ _ _ _ _ .
(B) Is it a fleshy fruit?

(A) No, it is not a _ _ _ _ _ _ _ _ _ _ .
(B) Is it a characteristic, or quality?

(A) Yes, it is a _ _ _ _ _ _ _ _ _ _ .

The next one is much harder because it deals with rhyming two-syllable words.

3. (A) I know a word that rhymes with *display*.
(B) Does it mean to comply with an order?

(A) No, it is not _ _ _ _ _ _ _ _ _ _ _ _ _ _ .
(B) Is it a bunch of flowers?

(A) No, it is not a _ _ _ _ _ _ _ _ _ _ _ _ _ _ .
(B) Is it a light, fluffy food made with eggs?

(A) No, it is not a _ _ _ _ _ _ _ _ _ _ _ _ _ _ .
(B) Is it a man's wig?

(A) Yes, it is a _ _ _ _ _ _ _ _ _ _ _ _ _ _ .

Here's a four-syllable poser. It's harder yet!

4. (A) I know a word that rhymes with *anticipate*.
(B) Does it mean to delay, to put off until later?

(A) No, it is not _ .
(B) Does it mean to make easier?

(A) No, it is not _ .
(B) Does it mean to discuss a problem to find terms suitable to opposing sides?

(A) No, it is not _ .
(B) Does it mean to make someone immune to a particular disease by means of an injection?

(A) Yes, it is _ .

Follow-up: Here are a few good starting words: *sardine, musketeer, eloquent, valentine.* Try them on your friends or at a party! You will enjoy it and will add new words to your daily vocabulary.

15. SYLLABLE STRUCTURES

Here's a game that will really make you think! You may not have realized it, but many words of two or more syllables are made up of monosyllabic words. In this game you are given definitions of syllables. If you identify the syllables correctly and combine them, you will arrive successfully at the whole word. (Note: The definitions given will help you to discover the *sound* of the syllables, not necessarily the spelling.)

Example:
the first syllable = to soar
the second syllable = part of a plant
the whole word = a blank sheet in the front or back of a book
Answer: fly + leaf = flyleaf

How many of the following can *you* solve?

1. _____ the first syllable = to stitch

   _____ the second syllable = base, vile

   _____ the whole word = a performance by one person

2. _____ the first syllable = a large boat, once used as a place of refuge

   _____ the second syllable = a facial spasm

   _____ the whole word = characteristic of the North Pole; frigid

3. _____ the first syllable = moved rapidly

   _____ the second syllable = a bag

   _____ the whole word = to search vigorously

4. _____ the first syllable = a young sheep

   _____ the second syllable = to moisten while roasting

   _____ the whole word = to beat severely

5. _____ the first syllable = to bring to a pier

   _____ the second syllable = second person pronoun

   _____ the third syllable = intended

   _____ the whole word = an official paper

6. _____ the first syllable = a male sheep

   _____ the second syllable = a boy attendant (e.g., in the Senate)

   _____ the whole word = violent behavior

7. _____ the first syllable = a short explosive sound

   _____ the second syllable = a common preposition

   _____ the third syllable = a bird with a loud, harsh call

   _____ the whole word = a vain, supercilious person

8. _____ the first syllable = a vessel used for drinking tea

   _____ the second syllable = lighted

   _____ the whole word = a two-line poem

9. _____ the first syllable = a piece of wire with a sharp point, used for fastening

   _____ the second syllable = a foot digit

   _____ the whole word = a horse with irregular spots

10. _____ the first syllable = a feline animal

    _____ the second syllable = the most often used article (one letter)

    _____ the third syllable = a catalogue of names or items

    _____ the whole word = a substance that causes a change in another substance

11. _____ the first syllable = a mongrel dog

    _____ the second syllable = not many but some

    _____ the whole word = a specified time when all unauthorized persons must
                                                  be off the streets

12. _____ the first syllable = arrived

    _____ the second syllable = a rectangular block of clay

    _____ the whole word = a cotton or linen fabric

13. _____ the first syllable = to strike hard; to butt

    _____ the second syllable = a piece

    _____ the whole word = a bulwark or defense

14. _____ the first syllable = a favorite kind of word play

    _____ the second syllable = a slangy abbreviation for a man

    _____ the whole word = biting; sharp to the taste

15. _____ the first syllable = a small particle of bread

    _____ the second syllable = a hole in the ground

    _____ the whole word = a small round cake of unsweetened batter cooked on a
                                                  griddle

16. _____ the first syllable = exist

_____ the second syllable = an unconscious part of the psyche

_____ the whole word = dull blue in color (said especially of a bruise)

17. _____ the first syllable = the sound of a contented cat

_____ the second syllable = first person pronoun, objective case

_____ the third syllable = devoured

_____ the whole word = to penetrate, to saturate

18. _____ the first syllable = a body of matter

_____ the second syllable = a petty quarrel

_____ the whole word = a stoutly built dog

16. CAN YOU THINK OF A WORD THAT . . . ?

This isn't really a game, but you will find it challenging. It is simply a series of questions about strange and interesting word structures. How many can you answer?

------------------------ 1. Can you think of a word that contains all five vowels in alphabetical order?

------------------------ 2. Can you think of an unusual seven-letter word that contains three u's?

------------------------ 3. Can you think of a word that ends in "full"?

4. The combination "ou" may be pronounced in the following ways: ou—ô—ō—ōō—ŏŏ—ŭ—û. (See the key at the bottom of the page.)

------------------------   *a.* Can you think of a word that means "to evict" and that begins with "ou" sounded as "ou"?

------------------------   *b.* Can you think of a word that means "to be obliged" and that begins with "ou" sounded as ô?

------------------------   *c.* Can you think of a word that means a branch of a tree, that begins with "b," and that includes "ou" sounded as "ou"?

------------------------   *d.* Can you think of a word that means "purchased," that begins with "b," and that includes "ou" sounded as ô?

------------------------   *e.* Can you think of a word that names a large, rounded rock, that begins with "b," and that includes "ou" sounded as ō?

------------------------   *f.* Can you think of a word that names a lady's private room, that begins with "b," and that includes "ou" sounded as ōō?

------------------------   *g.* Can you think of a word that is used to describe the middle class, that begins with "b," and that includes "ou" sounded as ŏŏ?

------------------------   *h.* Can you think of a word that names a two-line unit of verse, that begins with a "c," and that includes "ou" sounded as ŭ?

------------------------   *i.* Can you think of a word that means "politeness," that begins with a "c," and that includes "ou" sounded as û?

5. The combination "eu" is generally pronounced ū or yŏŏ or ōō.

------------------------   *a.* Can you think of a word that means "high praise" and that begins with "eu" sounded as ū?

------------------------   *b.* Can you think of a word that is an exclamation expressing triumph over a discovery and that begins with "eu" sounded as yŏŏ?

------------------------   *c.* Can you think of a word that denotes an abnormal condition of the blood, that begins with "l," and that includes "eu" sounded as ōō?

6. The combination "au" may be pronounced ô—ō—ă—ā.

------------------------   *a.* Can you think of a word used to describe the color of hair that begins with "au" sounded as ô?

------------------------   *b.* Can you think of a word beginning with "c" that uses the same "au" sound and that is used in politics?

Key: ăct, āble, ōver, ôrder, bŏŏk, ōōze, out, ŭp, ūse, ûrge

101 Ways to Learn Vocabulary

----------------------   c. Can you think of a word that names a relative and that begins with the "au" combination sounded as ă?

----------------------   d. Can you think of a word beginning with "g" that means clumsy, or awkward, and that includes "au" sounded as ō?

----------------------   e. Can you think of a word beginning with "g" that means to appraise, or estimate, and that uses "au" sounded as ā?

7. Some consonants just don't seem to go together, especially at the beginning of words; and yet, occasionally they do. How many of the following can you identify?

----------------------   *a.* a former Russian ruler that begins with "ts"

----------------------   *b.* bread sliced and toasted in an oven, beginning with "zw"

----------------------   *c.* a disease of the lungs, beginning with "pn"

----------------------   *d.* a light yellowish brown fabric, beginning with "kh"

----------------------   *e.* pertaining to spirit or mind, beginning with "ps"

----------------------   *f.* a type of food poisoning, beginning with "pt"

----------------------   *g.* a South American beast of burden, beginning with "ll"

----------------------   *h.* knotted, twisted, and rugged, beginning with "gn"

----------------------   *i.* a Hindu word, indicating essential quality of character, beginning with "dh"

----------------------   *j.* slender, beginning with "sv"

----------------------   *k.* intended to aid the memory, beginning with "mn"

17. PRESIDENTIAL PARLAY

Starting with George Washington, the United States has had thirty-seven Presidents. Their names are listed below.

George Washington	Franklin Pierce	Theodore Roosevelt
John Adams	James Buchanan	William H. Taft
Thomas Jefferson	Abraham Lincoln	Woodrow Wilson
James Madison	Andrew Johnson	Warren G. Harding
James Monroe	Ulysses S. Grant	Calvin Coolidge
John Quincy Adams	Rutherford B. Hayes	Herbert C. Hoover
Andrew Jackson	James A. Garfield	Franklin D. Roosevelt
Martin Van Buren	Chester A. Arthur	Harry S. Truman
William Henry Harrison	Grover Cleveland	Dwight D. Eisenhower
John Tyler	Benjamin Harrison	John F. Kennedy
James K. Polk	Grover Cleveland	Lyndon B. Johnson
Zachary Taylor	William McKinley	Richard M. Nixon
Millard Fillmore		

If we look closely at these presidential names and analyze them, we can find all sorts of hidden word treasure!

I. First, some presidential names (first, middle, or last) have a specific meaning as independent words.

> *Example:* A large covered truck for transporting goods is called a _ _ _ _ _ _ .
> *Answer:* Martin *Van* Buren

Can you find a presidential name to complete the following sentences?

1. A gift of money or land, given for a specific purpose, is called a _ _ _ _ _ _ _ _ _ _ _ _ _ _ _ _ .

2. A piece of ground reserved for the breeding of rabbits is called a _ _ _ _ _ _ _ _ _ _ _ _ _ _ _ .

3. A bird that resembles the swallow is called a _ _ _ _ _ _ _ _ _ _ _ _ _ _ _ .

4. A country gentleman or a property owner of nonnoble birth in England is called a _ _ _ _ _ _ _ _
   _ _ _ _ _ _ _ _ .

5. To cut or perforate is to _ _ _ _ _ _ _ _ _ _ _ _ _ _ _ .

II. Second, we can find hidden words.

> *Example:* In which presidential name can you find food for a horse?
> *Answer:* Rutherford B. *Hay*es

Now you try it. In which presidential name can you find

_ _ _ _ _ _ _ _ _ _ _ _ _ 1. fish eggs?

_ _ _ _ _ _ _ _ _ _ _ _ _ 2. a word meaning "candid"?

_ _ _ _ _ _ _ _ _ _ _ _ _ 3. a preserve?

_ _ _ _ _ _ _ _ _ _ _ _ _ 4. a farmyard bird?

101 Ways to Learn Vocabulary

------------- 5. laundry?

------------- 6. a word meaning "rabid"?

------------- 7. a word meaning "sketched"?

------------- 8. a group of trees?

------------- 9. relatives?

------------- 10. barriers holding back water?

------------- 11. an open expanse of land?

------------- 12. a word meaning "to burn the surface of"?

------------- 13. a shallow place in a river where a crossing can be made?

------------- 14. a word meaning "wealthy"?

------------- 15. the grayish-white residue of combustion?

------------- 16. a word meaning "to damage or deface"?

------------- 17. a building intended to grind grain into flour?

------------- 18. a structure built to serve as a docking place for ships?

------------- 19. a relative position in society; or an official grade?

------------- 20. a word meaning "to tear down to the ground; to raze"?

Something new to try: Make a list of the names of relatives or friends and see how many hidden words or independent words you can detect. Then, test *them!*

18. DAISY CHAIN

Link the end of one word to the beginning of the next—into a chain of six "daisies." This game is possible because many words in English are really a combination of two simple words. Two such words are "lock*jaw*" and "*jaw*breaker."

In this game you are given six definitions. If you can find the words that fit the definitions, you will end up with a "chain."

Example:

daisy chain	enlaced flowers
chain letter	epistle sent from person A to B, from B to C, etc.
letterhead	stationery with a printed heading
headrest	a support for the head
rest cure	treatment for nervous disorders
cure-all	panacea

Note that the two-part terms may be written as solid compounds, may be hyphenated, or may be composed of two distinct words. Note also that when all the correct words are inserted, the last part of one term is the first part of the following term. You can begin anywhere on the chain and work up or down, as you like.

Here are four "daisy chains" for you to tackle.

1. _____ a type of thief

   _____ a knife that folds

   _____ something very sharp

   _____ sideways

   _____ a facetious remark

   _____ an eccentric person

2. _____ a type of hotel employee

   _____ a member of a youth organization

   _____ the leader in charge of this youth organization

   _____ a work done with extraordinary skill

   _____ work paid for at a rate based on the number of articles made

   _____ exercise to improve one's fitness for athletic competition

3. _____ a destructive rush of water, due to heavy rains

   _____ a projector that gives a bright, broad beam of light

   _____ a tower that guides mariners

   _____ a party lasting one or more nights at a residence

   _____ announced policies of a political group

   _____ a commissioned officer assigned to the line

4.   ---------------------- a sorcerer, or wizard

---------------------- closing of a business by the employer because of a conflict with employees

---------------------- a riot, or insurrection

---------------------- disintegration or dispersal

---------------------- the act of maintaining in good condition

---------------------- something kept or given as a memento

19. A GAGGLE OF GUESSING GAMES

Everybody likes to play guessing games. The ones below you can play by yourself, but they can easily be adapted to play with friends.

I. In this game you are given several hints. See how fast you can guess the answer.

> *Example:* This word has six letters.
> It begins with a "b."
> It may relate to a river, the nose, or cards.
> *Answer:* bridge

Here are some for you to guess.

- - - - - - - - - - - - 1. This word has four letters.
It begins with an "h."
It may refer to a residence, an institution, or a baseball plate.

- - - - - - - - - - - - 2. This word has four letters.
It begins with a "j."
It may refer to trash or a Chinese boat.

- - - - - - - - - - - - 3. This word has four letters.
It begins with an "l."
It may refer to a bird or a prank.

- - - - - - - - - - - - 4. This word has six letters.
It begins with an "n."
It may relate to teasing, a pine tree, or sewing.

- - - - - - - - - - - - 5. This word has five letters.
It begins with a "p."
It may refer to a political group or a social affair.

II. This guessing game is all about trees. Are you a tree-lover? How many trees can you find by following these nonsense clues?

> *Example:* not me but - - - - - -
> *Answer:* yew

Ready?

- - - - - - - - - - - 1. a place for swimming

- - - - - - - - - - - 2. It yearns a lot.

- - - - - - - - - - - 3. fire's end

- - - - - - - - - - - 4. branch, drab, or oil

- - - - - - - - - - - 5. neat as a pin

- - - - - - - - - - - 6. the under part of the hand

- - - - - - - - - - - 7. presidential tree, 1964–1968

101 Ways to Learn Vocabulary

---------- 8. not younger

---------- 9. Egypt's old plague

---------- 10. Saturday night

III. And this guessing game is all about birds. How many birds can you find by following these nonsense clues?

> *Example:* a vain person
> *Answer:* peacock

------------------ 1. a braggart

------------------ 2. a high ecclesiastic

------------------ 3. Hard ball! Get out of the way!

------------------ 4. refuses to face reality

------------------ 5. a gulp

------------------ 6. a foot racer

------------------ 7. a mimicker

------------------ 8. an eccentric

------------------ 9. an informer

------------------ 10. flies at the end of a string

IV. In this guessing game you are given five clues. If you guess the word after the first clue, give yourself 10 points; after the second clue, 8 points; after the third clue, 6 points; after the fourth clue, 4 points; after the fifth clue, 2 points.

Example:
  a. This word has five letters and is one of the seven deadly sins.
  b. It can also be used to describe a group of lions.
  c. It is a one-syllable word and rhymes with *cried*.
  d. It sometimes describes the "best," the elite.
  e. As an adjective, it means *arrogant, conceited*.
Answer: pride

  How high can you score on the following?

1. *a.* This word has ten letters and, as a noun, is a plate of type metal.
  b. It has four syllables; the first three syllables are popular in sound systems.
  c. The last syllable refers to mechanical writing.
  d. It can mean a conventional, over-simplified opinion.
  e. It most often describes someone who possesses the characteristics of a certain type of person.

  Answer: ------------------------

2. *a.* This word has eleven letters and is a favorite with today's young people.
   b. It has four syllables; the third rhymes with "bell."
   c. The first two syllables come from the Greek word meaning "soul," or "spirit."
   d. It is often used as an adjective describing a particular kind of modern experience.
   e. This word is usually associated with flashing colors, erratic movement, and confusing images.

   Answer: _____

3. *a.* This word has twelve letters and can mean "unspoken."
   b. It has five syllables; the third is the sound of a clock.
   c. In zoology it means "not segmented," as with certain worms.
   d. The last syllable *looks* as though it should rhyme with *date*.
   e. Its most usual use is as an adjective describing a person who has difficulty expressing himself.

   Answer: _____

20. FIVE FIVE-MINUTE FILLERS

Here are several very short games. To make them more interesting, time yourself. Give yourself only *five* minutes to complete each game.

I. Choose any two consecutive letters in the alphabet—for example, *c* and *d*. Then make a word by inserting *one* letter between them. By inserting "a" between *c* and *d*, you can form the word *cad*.

Now go through the alphabet and see if you can form ten words, each from a different pair of consecutive letters. (You may use *c* and *d*, but you must insert a different letter between them!)

------   ------

------   ------

------   ------

------   ------

------   ------

II. It is possible (but not easy) to find *three* consecutive letters of the alphabet, *in order*, in a word. For example, *s t u* are consecutive, and you can find these letters, in order, in the word "*stu*nt." Can you discover five more words, each with a different three-letter combination?

----------------   ----------------

----------------   ----------------

III. Not many English words end in a single "f." One exception is "if." Another is "dwarf." Can you find twenty more words ending in a single "f"? In five minutes, of course!

----------   ----------   ----------   ----------

----------   ----------   ----------   ----------

----------   ----------   ----------   ----------

----------   ----------   ----------   ----------

----------   ----------   ----------   ----------

IV. Using the letters in the square below, try to make at least thirty-five words by moving up, down, to right, or to left through adjoining boxes. For example, starting in the right-hand top corner, you can begin with "F," move left to "A," then down to "D" for the word *fad*. Remember— you have only five minutes!

A	L	A	F
R	E	D	I
O	P	O	N
T	A	G	E

---------   ---------   ---------   ---------   ---------
---------   ---------   ---------   ---------   ---------
---------   ---------   ---------   ---------   ---------
---------   ---------   ---------   ---------   ---------
---------   ---------   ---------   ---------   ---------
---------   ---------   ---------   ---------   ---------
---------   ---------   ---------   ---------   ---------

V. Moving clockwise (left to right) on the circle below, try to find at least twenty words without skipping any boxes. For example, starting at the top of the circle, the first letter is *d*, the second is *o*; together, they form the word *do*. Again—remember your five-minute deadline.

----------   ----------   ----------   ----------   ----------
----------   ----------   ----------   ----------   ----------
----------   ----------   ----------   ----------   ----------
----------   ----------   ----------   ----------   ----------
----------   ----------   ----------   ----------   ----------

LESSON 101

WORD-A-DAY

As you have seen—in one hundred different ways in the preceding lessons—words are fascinating, useful, and powerful. Collectively, they are the most important key to communication. Without them, you are almost helpless. With them, you can express your emotions, clarify your ideas, and change the opinions of others. They are a kind of Aladdin's magic lamp!

The final question, then, is: *How can you continue to stock your storehouse of words?*

And the final answer is: *By the "word-a-day" plan.*

Here's how it works:

1. Select one word each day. It should preferably be a word that is relevant and significant. During a presidential election it might be "electoral" or "plurality" or "affiliation." (Best sources: newspapers, weekly news magazines, television documentaries.)

2. Next learn the word thoroughly. Learn the exact meaning of the word. If there are several meanings, learn all that are in common usage. And learn to pronounce the word correctly and easily.

3. Now *use* the word, not once but at least five times during the day. Use it in speech and use it in writing. Use it seriously and use it facetiously. Use it with teachers and parents and friends. Use it in daydreams and in your thinking. *Listen* for it—in the speech of others and as you watch television. *Look* for it—in newspapers, advertisements, and magazines. By the end of the day, the new word should be thoroughly familiar, an additional tool in your semantics kit. By the end of the year, you will have 365 such tools, all sharp-edged and ready for use.

The Group Plan

You can expand "word-a-day" by employing the group plan. You can organize a few willing friends, your English class, or even—if enough people are interested—your entire school. Below are some suggestions for the organization and operation of the group approach.

1. Form a committee of friends, or of students and teachers, depending on the group involved.

2. Each day one member of the committee chooses one word.

3. Each morning, before school begins, place a poster in the classroom, or (if the entire school is involved) near the main doors. Each poster should contain—in large, easily read letters—the word for the day.

4. Try to insert the word (correctly used, of course!) in the announcements that go over the public address system during homeroom.

5. Ask teachers of all subject-matter classes to use the word as often as possible during classes. Encourage students to use the word in class and out of class.

6. Enlist the aid of the editor of the school newspaper. Ask him to use as many of the words as possible in the current edition of the newspaper.

7. Set up one-day shows on a bulletin board or in a display case. Keep the exhibits small, simple, and dramatic. Aim often for humor: cartoons, jokes, abstractions, light verse. But keep firmly centered, always, the word for the day.

8. Vary the types of words chosen. If a word from politics is used one day, choose for the next day one from science or the entertainment world. But whatever words are finally selected, be sure they are really useful—words that all students can begin using at once, and continue using.

The "word-a-day" plan works best with a group. Shared, it is more fun and probably more memorable. But it will work for an individual; it will work for *you*. Best of all, it can become a permanent habit, an enduring contributor to your intellectual growth. Recognizing no school holidays, never ending with a graduation ceremony, it can be a lifelong friend—providing the words with which to form thoughts, the words by which you can express those thoughts, the words with which you can share those thoughts with others. Words are a key not only to communication; through communication, they are a key, also, to the mind and heart of your fellowman.

Index